and the
Giant Cat
For Gerald, Murray, Barry, Craig, and Shari

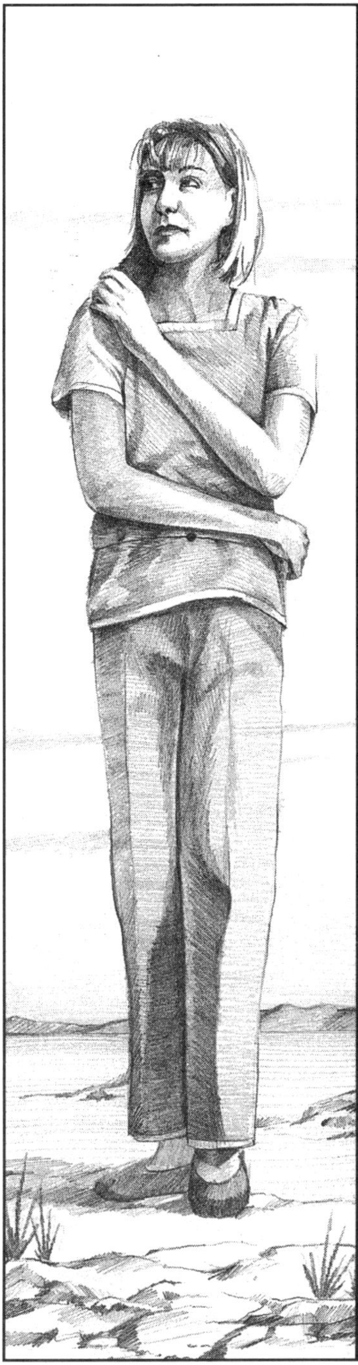

CONTENTS

CHAPTER 1

C'Off

"Next!"

The C'Off was bored. How many more of these Y'Ads could be left for him to see? Six? Sixty? Six hundred? And every one of them had to be placed in an appropriate job by the end of the week! Of course, in most cases, the real work would be performed by a BOSS, but AusLaw said all Y'Ads had to have jobs within a week of leaving school, presumably to keep them out of mischief. AusLaw didn't waste time and it didn't allow the C'Off to waste it either.

The C'Off closed his eyes. The job might have been entertaining if *he'd* been able to match available Y'Ads to available opportunities. Unfortunately, all the matches were premade by a BOSS, and all the C'Off could do was give the news to the Y'Ads concerned. He wouldn't have been able to do *that* if not for PHT, or Project Human Touch, as AusLaw called it. Without PHT, the news could just as well have been sent to the Y'Ads by e-mail.

The C'Off's eyes were closed for only five seconds, but when he opened them again, he found himself facing yet another Y'Ad. This one was female, tall and thin, with short brown hair, a large nose, and a pair of bright brown eyes that seemed to take in everything. She was wearing the universal Y'Ad uniform of loose brown trousers and a shapeless brown tunic. These garments were issued to all Y'Ads by AusLaw, two sets twice a year, or more often if a set was damaged or if the recipient grew a great deal. Everyone wore the same uniforms, only the colors differed.

Orange for Kids
Green for Pr'Ads
Brown for Y'Ads
Red for M'Ads
Blue for Sen'Cits
Yellow for Elds

Kids, Pr'Ads, Y'Ads, M'Ads, Sen'Cits, and Elds.

Orange, green, brown, red, blue, and yellow.

It was a good system. The C'Off liked it. It helped him remember who was who and how much respect had to be shown to each individual. Only, he wasn't fond of brown. He'd been very relieved when he'd been able to exchange his own brown uniform for the red uniform of a M'Ad, and trade his last make-work occupation for... well, another of the same.

"Name?" The C'Off yawned. He didn't care what her name was. They all looked alike, they all sounded alike, and they all behaved alike. They were Y'Ads. Once, in the Days of Waste, they'd been known as teenagers. Now they were Y'Ads. Who cared? They were still a nuisance.

"I'm CD." She had a soft voice, and he didn't care what she was called, but he had his job to do.

"CD?" The C'Off yawned again.

"Uhm, Callista Derry," the Y'Ad answered.

"Well, how do you like being a Y'Ad, Callista Derry?" It was another mechanical question, one he asked every graduate.

She shrugged and smiled. "I guess it's not that much different from being a Pr'Ad so far. Except I'm thirteen instead of twelve, and of course I now have a pet license! I'm going to have a cat!"

Her face lit up with delight, but the C'Off held up a hand to stop her. He wasn't interested in cats. He wasn't interested in the Y'Ad. He wasn't even interested in his job, but it had to be done. After all, AusLaw had made PHT a priority.

"So now you're ready to work," he said, forcing himself to smile. "I'm glad to tell you we have just the position for you, CV!"

"CD," she corrected gently.

"*CD*. Of course. We have just the position for you!" he repeated, sneaking a glance at his cue-screen, then trying to mask a look of utter astonishment. AusLaw was sending her *there?* What on Earth had this Y'Ad done? "I believe that you requested work with either music or animals?" he stammered.

Her face lit up again. "Oh yes! What did I get? Balladry? Stage work? Vet training?"

"None of the above," the C'Off said curtly. "Isolated hospitality and service."

"Oh?" she said.

"You will spend the next year working at Desert Depot. Please report there early tomorrow morning by jet-carrier. Next!"

The C'Off closed his eyes, willing the Y'Ad to go away, but when he opened them she was still there. "Off you go, CD," he snapped.

"But I really don't understand at all," she said finally. "Where and what is Desert Depot? I thought I'd be working in the city."

"Desert Depot is a service center in the Great Stone Desert," the C'Off read from the cue-screen. "Tourist solar-buses stop there to rehydrate." He looked up and added, "It's run by a BOSS, of course, but with PHT in force, I suppose AusLaw wants a human present to welcome the tourists." His mouth twisted. Who would ever want to go touring in the Great Stone Desert? There was nothing there but, well, rocks!

"But what does any of that have to do with music or animals?" she asked, obviously perplexed.

"One of your tasks will be to oversee the production of juke-discs," he said inventively, "and I believe there are still some thorn lizards in the area. Next!"

CD caught the speed-rail home.

"Well, Callista?" said her mother, Ashlin. "What did you get?"

"Isolated hospitality at Desert Depot," said CD. She was so disappointed she could have cried. "It's out in the Great Stone Desert."

"Well, *that's* different," said Ashlin, with the air of someone trying to understand the impossible. How *could* her lovely daughter, bright, kind, friendly, and creative, have been given such a job?

CD managed to smile. "Different, but not at all what I wanted. I'll get to see a thorn lizard if I'm lucky, and I can put together juke-discs to suit other people. I might just as well be a BOSS. Mom, why would AusLaw send me there? I haven't done anything bad. I haven't!"

"Of course not. You would have been notified." Ashlin spoke bracingly. There was nothing she could do, though. AusLaw said Y'Ads must be provided with suitable jobs within a week of leaving school. It didn't say they had to like them.

"It isn't fair," said CD.

"Well, I suppose there was a vacancy there and your name came up," said Ashlin.

"Maybe. But why can't we choose what we want to do the way Grandad Derry's great-grandad did?"

"Because we might all choose the same thing, and that wouldn't work at all," said Ashlin briskly. "Think of it – five hundred Policam-Assistants, but not a single Hydroponic-Monitor!"

"Oh well, at least I can order my clone-kit now," said CD. "What sort of cat do you think I should get?"

"A ragdoll," said her mother. "They're by far the most obedient."

CD frowned. "I would really prefer to have a friend, not a slave."

"All right," said Ashlin. "It's your choice." She smiled a little sadly. It was probably the only real free choice her daughter would ever be allowed to make. "It's your right to have a domestic pet, but it's also your responsibility!" she added. "Now go to bed, Callista. You'll be busy in the morning."

"Busy at Desert Depot," said CD a bit grimly. "Goodnight, Mom." She reached out and tugged her mother's long braid. CD knew it was a childish habit for a Y'Ad, but it was one she hadn't yet discarded.

"Goodnight, Callista," said Ashlin. "How strange, this is the last time I will ever send you to bed!"

CD snapped her fingers. "I *knew* there had to be some advantage to being a Y'Ad!"

She laughed and went to bed, but Ashlin couldn't help wondering just how busy her daughter would really be. AusLaw said a lot about creating jobs for Y'Ads, but none of the jobs seemed to involve much activity. CD would be welcoming tourists to the desert. That sounded fine, but did tourists ever *go* to the desert? Ashlin had her doubts. Most of the people she knew jetted *over* the desert at the height of 5,000 meters and at such speeds that the earth was a blur beneath them. Why would they want to land? There was nothing to see but brush and rocks, and nothing to do but sweat. Tourism wasn't exactly encouraged in the desert anyway. Like every other type of natural environment, the Great Stone Desert was fiercely protected by AusLaw.

As far as Ashlin could tell, AusLaw had simply tucked the girl safely out of the way of anything she might enjoy. Ashlin shrugged. That was life, and at least Callista had her music and could look forward to ordering her pet. And with vidwindows, the isolation factor would not be deemed a hardship by AusLaw.

Ashlin sighed. Vidwindows allowed free real-time communication, and perfect audiovisuals, but they didn't allow for hugs.

CHAPTER 2

Desert Depot

CD looked out the window of her sleeping quarters on the 157th floor of the highriser in which she and her parents lived. It was the last time she would see this view for a year, so she scanned it with renewed attention.

Large belts of tall trees divided the entire city in a checkerboard shape, and each highriser stood in its own green neighborhood. The sky was brilliantly blue and clear. It hadn't always been like that. Her grandfather, Galway Derry, remembered his own great-grandfather telling him about a sky full of smog, treeless cities, and ground traffic slowed to a crawl. That had been way back in the last Days of Waste. A few people called that era the Days of Freedom, but they were making a wry comment on the excesses of the past. What they meant was that people had the freedom to pollute the planet and use up resources, the freedom to waste food and time and lives, and the freedom to argue with one another while most real problems went unsolved. As Galway Derry always noted, this latter freedom was practiced particularly by politicians.

That was all over, and now AusLaw made sure everyone had enough food to eat and clothes to wear. AusLaw also provided everyone with a basic education, a place to live, and anything else they needed. In return, people did as they were told. Kids were under the authority of their parents. Pr'Ads obeyed at school. Y'Ads and M'Ads worked directly under BOSSes representing AusLaw, and Elds were sheltered in complexes. Only Sen'Cits had any real degree of spare time, and most of them didn't bother to use it.

"You win some, you lose some," said Galway. "Maybe one day we'll all be trusted with freedom of choice again."

"We'd probably just mess it up again," said CD.

The new speed-rails webbed the city above and below, and the streets had been replaced by a system of parks and lawns. Nobody owned an individual vehicle, and nobody owned any land. AusLaw's great megachip brain decided what to build and when to build it, as well as what should be torn down to make way.

"My great-grandad would say the city's lost all of its character," said Galway, but he still had to admit it was a pleasant place to live. Fresh air, trees, flowers, and communal gardens were everywhere, crisscrossed by landscaped trails for the compulsory exercise everyone had to take. Yes, the city was a nice place. Most people liked it very much, and those who didn't, left. Away from the city, they had to spend so much more time fending for themselves that most of them soon returned.

Galway apparently had no desire to leave the city, for though he was now a Sen'Cit, and officially free to go where he chose and still draw his rations and necessities, he spent most of the time in the gardens of the highriser in which he lived. CD had always loved to spend time with him there, listening to his stories, but from now on it would be very difficult to find any opportunity to see him at all.

"I'm going to miss Grandad Derry," she said as Ashlin hurried into the room.

"I know," said Ashlin. "But you shouldn't take *too* much notice of his tales, Callista. He loves to talk. He could talk all day and all night if he wanted. Come to think of it, he *does*, but you can't." Ashlin sighed. "Sometimes, I think the Sen'Cits are the lucky ones. No duties, no worries. Bliss!"

"Sorry, Mom," said CD with a grin. "You have about another twenty years to go."

"Don't remind me." Ashlin rested her hand on her daughter's shoulder. "Well, Callista, it's time to go. The jet-carrier's waiting for you, and I must get to work."

"Of course," said CD. "See you next year!" She kept her smile pinned in place until her mother had gone.

Twenty minutes later, CD scrambled out of the jet-carrier and hitched her gear onto her shoulder. Her first sight of her new home didn't do much to lift her spirits. Not an animal stirred. Not a note of music could be heard. CD whistled a tune, but her lips were dry in the desert air and the thin melody was swallowed up in the silence. In the city, the tune would have been taken up by half a dozen Pr'Ads, but here there was only the wind.

AUS

The Great Stone Desert was large and flat and hot, and the ground was covered with brush and rock in roughly equal amounts. An occasional bone proved that some small animal or bird had given up living in the desert. CD took a few steps forward and stumbled over a rock. "Politicians!" she swore, but the word made no more impression on the desert than her whistling had.

Actually, thought CD, it would be very difficult to make an impression on the desert. She wondered if she would even bother to try. What could she have *done?* Of course, she was at liberty to ask AusLaw about her record, but AusLaw was at liberty to not answer. "AusLaw stinks," said CD, grinning. She could say what she liked about AusLaw as long as she didn't *do* anything against it. AusLaw didn't care what Y'Ads thought or said, only what they did.

The only smooth surface in sight was the road, which looked hot, dry, and dusty. The only change of color came from the sky and the white plasticrete domes of Desert Depot. Behind the domes was a large solar-bus parking lot. Apart from the jet-carrier from which CD had just emerged, the parking lot was empty, and apart from Desert Depot, so was the desert. There were no hills, no water, no trees, no animals, and no people – just rocks and dry vegetation.

"Where is everyone?" asked CD.

The pilot of the jet-carrier didn't answer. He was a service BOSS with a low-input vocabulary, and he wasn't prepared to waste any of it on an insignificant Y'Ad, especially one who effectively had been banished from the city. The human copilot was asleep. That didn't matter. Even if he had been able to fly the jet-carrier, he wouldn't have been expected to do so. His only duty was to be there.

"I suppose the other Y'Ads are all inside Desert Depot," said CD, answering herself. "They're probably preparing to welcome the next batch of tourists."

But where *were* the tourists?

Baffled, she looked around. No solar-buses. And no people. "Oh well," said CD. "It's still early. I guess the tourists will be pouring in by lunchtime." She tried to believe it would happen.

The jet-carrier took off back to the city and CD stood alone in the silence. Her bundle of belongings was small and light because everything she needed would be provided at Desert Depot. The toys and clothes she had had as a Pr'Ad had been reclaimed by AusLaw, for redistribution to the next crop of Pr'Ads. In exchange, she had been issued new clothes, a musical instrument, and a data-disc, as well as a duty manual that explained her new status and responsibilities as a Y'Ad. She was wearing the clothes and looked forward to playing the instrument – a guitar – and reading from the data-disc. As far as she was concerned, the manual could stay in her bundle. It had certainly been written by a BOSS.

CD glanced at the white domes and then at the hazy horizon. "I wonder what would happen if I just started walking," she said aloud. "Would anyone try to stop me?"

There was no reply. The desert seemed empty, bare of policam security surveillance, but you never knew.

There was a good chance that someone in the city was watching every move she made and hearing every word she spoke. CD looked around again. She still couldn't see any policams, but that didn't mean they weren't there. She didn't always see them in the city either, but they always saw her, and they kept her safe. CD gave a friendly wave, just in case.

The idea of security cameras had been around for centuries, but it was only during the past hundred years that they had been used so extensively. Now every city corner and every city building was under permanent, twenty-four-hour scrutiny.

CD hardly ever thought about the policams, because she couldn't remember anything else, but her grandfather had frightening stories to tell of the time before AusLaw had started using the policams.

"When my great-grandfather was a boy, it wouldn't have been safe for you to walk down the street at night, Callie," said Galway, using his pet name for her. "There was very little protection or security, so you might have been mugged or assaulted at any time."

"What's mugged?"

"Someone beats you up and then takes away all of your belongings."

CD couldn't see the point in that. Who would want *her* belongings? All citizens had their own. "What's assaulted, then?"

"Being hit and hurt and frightened by someone. Some people did it to make themselves feel better at another person's expense."

"Weird," said CD.

"It couldn't happen now," said Galway reassuringly. "Not with the policams. One aggressive move and you wake up an hour later with a headache from the sleepygas. A few doses of sleepygas, and most people learn not to make aggressive moves. The world's a safer place these days, and we have a lot to be thankful for."

CD was very thankful, so she always waved to the policams when she saw them. AusLaw insisted that each policam be paired with a human assistant, and since the assistants had nothing to do except make sure the policams were working well, they did get bored. CD's dad was a Policam-Assistant, and he said he listened to music most of the time, but he also said he was always happy to see a friendly smile. Since CD never knew which policam was paired with her dad, she smiled at all of them.

Stepping carefully, CD turned her back on Desert Depot and walked several hundred meters out into the desert. As far as the policams were concerned – if there *were* any policams out here – she could have kept walking until she reached the ocean. Of course, she would have to turn back and return to work in the end. If she were gone for six months, her year of duty at Desert Depot would simply start and end six months later. She would still serve a year, so why put it off? And of course she wouldn't be issued food or clothes during any period that she wasn't at work.

She stopped walking and rested one foot on a large hunk of rock. A spot between her shoulder blades began to itch, and she wriggled her shoulders and reached around to rub the spot. Her fingertips felt nothing unusual, but the sensation persisted. Despite the heat, there seemed to be a chill spreading up her spine, as if someone were watching her.

It might be a telescopic policam, but she didn't think so. She was used to them, and they never made her uneasy.

There was no one around, so CD decided it was the emptiness of the desert oppressing her. She was used to an orderly green landscape, well-populated with Pr'Ads, Y'Ads, M'Ads, and Sen'Cits, with the occasional Kid or Eld. This landscape wasn't at all green, and seemed as unpopulated as it could get now that the jet-carrier had left. CD decided to go into Desert Depot and find her fellow Y'Ad workers before she started imagining things.

As she turned back toward Desert Depot, she thought she saw a flicker of movement out on her right. She spun around, but there was nothing but brush and large chunks of tawny rock. "Is anyone out there?" she called.

It seemed possible that other Y'Ads were coming to welcome her, but if so, they were being very quiet. She waited for an answer or more movement, but neither came. Finally, CD decided it had probably been a small dust devil, or maybe a thorn lizard. Later, after she'd settled in, she would come back out to look. She wondered if a thorn lizard would make a good friend.

The back of her neck began to tingle again, but CD shrugged her shoulders and went into Desert Depot to find the other Y'Ads.

CHAPTER 3

BOSS

CD stood on the threshold of Desert Depot and faced the BOSS. It was an old Mark-17 model, with a shiny steel blue cranium and a holographic screen. The BOSS had four highly flexible limbs with grasping tools, and possessed a visual voice-sync so that when it spoke, its speech pattern was matched by the play of light across the screen that served the BOSS for a face.

<I am the BOSS.> said the BOSS. <BOSS is an acronym for Bio Over-SeerS.>

"Hi there," CD said. "Are you in charge of the Y'Ads who work here?"

<You are?>

"Callista Derry, Y'Ad. CD, if you prefer." CD focused her eyes on the BOSS's screen receptor so it could read her retinal print and register her identification. "Where are the other Y'Ads, BOSS?"

<Y'Ad Callista Derry is the sole human presence.>

CD's spirits sank. "In this room, or in the entire Desert Depot?" she asked with dread.

<Y'Ad Callista Derry is the sole human presence.>

"Politicians!" swore CD. "What *could* I have done to deserve this?" Hurriedly, she reviewed her school career. Nothing offered itself. She had worked very hard at school

and done well, and she had *never* been sleepygassed. Not once.

Putting down her bundle, CD shrugged. It was a bit unusual and unwelcome to send a Y'Ad to work alone in the middle of a desert, but not illegal. Of course it wasn't. AusLaw *was* the law, so whatever it did was legal.

"Where are the policams?" CD asked, glancing up at the white plasticrete walls and ceiling.

<Policams are in the city.>

"Yes, but where are they here? I can't see any lenses."

<Policams are in the city.>

"You mean there are no policams here at *all?*" It was a frightening thought.

<Correct.> said the BOSS.

"So," said CD, trying to suppress a shiver, "we're on our own until my pet arrives, which will be as soon as I've made a final decision about the breed. Would you tell me where my quarters are?"

The BOSS stretched out an appendage and indicated a door. CD picked up her bundle and went in.

The room was exactly like the one she had occupied at home. That was no real surprise – *all* Pr'Ad and Y'Ad quarters had the same pattern. There was a bed, a terminal, a small bathroom cubicle, a clothes chest, a vidwindow, and a sanitized recess area for a pet. The walls and ceiling were a soft shade of cream and gently curved.

CD put her guitar on the bed and opened her pack, preparing to make herself at home. It didn't take long.

Her spare set of clothing went in the clothes chest, her data-disc in the terminal, and the Y'Ad duty manual in the bottom drawer of the clothes chest. CD then turned her attention to her most cherished possession: a set of holo-posters showing the different available breeds of cats. Carefully, CD mounted them on the walls, then stood back to admire the effect.

There were six breeds currently available as domestic pets, all of them clone species with yellow or blue eyes. Once again, CD reviewed the Siamese, the Russian blue, the ragdoll, the Manx, the rex, and the Persian. Each was appealing in its own way, and she still couldn't quite make up her mind which one she should choose. The Siamese and the rex had an angular beauty, the Manx had an honest face, and the remaining three had flat faces and long, soft coats, but would require more grooming.

Her mother was in favor of the placid ragdoll, but CD was looking for something other than a fluffy toy. She wanted a friend. The Siamese and the Manx looked the most intelligent, but Siamese were known for their strong wills. It would probably be difficult for a Y'Ad to obtain a Siamese, and true Manxes were rare. For some reason, the cloning technique didn't always work very well, and mutations occurred.

CD looked over the selection again. Her choice, when she finally registered it with AusLaw, would be permanent. A Y'Ad had just one chance with a pet. The animals provided were healthy, hardy, and immune to most diseases. AusLaw supplied appropriate food, but providing exercise, cleanliness, play, and bonding was the responsibility of the Y'Ad. It was a serious decision, and one that could not be hurried. At least the posters were a comfort to have around.

CD patted her current favorite, the rex holo-poster, then went to find the BOSS. She had come to Desert Depot to work, and it was time to begin.

The BOSS was waiting where she had left it.

"I'm ready to start, BOSS," said CD. "Where do I go to begin?"

<Y'Ad Callista Derry is to proceed to souvenir center.> said the BOSS, extending an appendage to point the way.

Desert Depot was really quite large.

Apart from the solar-bus parking lot, everything was contained under the plasticrete domes. CD discovered the rehydrating station, where the vast water tanks stored enough liquid to rehydrate fifty solar-buses a day. Much smaller recycling barrels supplied the rest of Desert Depot, and there were separate holding tanks for the hydroponics gardens. These were contained in a small, separate dome and looked very interesting, but the entrance was electronically barred.

"Will I be working in there?" asked CD hopefully.

<Human assistance not currently required in garden center. Hydroponics off-limits to Y'Ad Callista Derry.>

That was a pity. CD liked plants. Ashlin worked as a Garden-Observer, and CD had sometimes watched. Of course, the Mark-27 BOSS was in charge of the garden and did most of the work, but Ashlin had picked up quite a bit of useful knowledge that she planned to put on a data-disc when she became a Sen'Cit.

The next section contained the overnighting tourist quarters. These were all empty. "How often do we have overnighters?" asked CD.

<Never.>

"Then why do we have the quarters?"

<Paradox.> remarked the BOSS, which was true, but not very helpful.

The souvenir and music centers were at the rear of the complex, and for the first time, CD felt a slight stirring of real hope. The entire souvenir center was crammed full of holo-posters, solar-hats, data-discs, histo-pics, promofilms, playing cards, drinking mugs, and autoflutes, and the music center contained the very latest JDM, or Juke-Disc-Mix equipment.

CD stared at the JDM in wonder for a few moments and then began to scroll through the choices. There were

ten thousand of them, ranging from ancient classical music right through jazz, folk, pop, and rock of the 20th century; then lift, bang, creezy, and natch of the 21st century; and the very latest in whalesong and graveldisc. There was catsong, sonicboom, subsonic and supersonic harmony, hushmusic, cloudmusic, melodiscs, and spheretune, and practically every other kind of music that had ever been recorded.

No, thought CD. Not *practically* every kind. It had *every* kind.

She felt a grin spreading over her face and drew in a deep breath. The C'Off had badly understated the case when he'd mentioned creating juke-discs! It was worth spending a year in the desert just to have the use of this JDM. A year would hardly be time enough to familiarize herself with the choices.

CD quickly accessed the ten sample juke-discs, already stamped with ten tracks each: ten classics, ten rock, ten hushmusic, ten subsonics, and ten whalesong. Whoever had mixed these juke-discs obviously had possessed no originality at all. The sample juke-discs were all so boring and predictable, CD itched to wipe them clear and produce some new mixes of her own.

She had her hand on the JDM's recycler when the BOSS rolled up.

<No unauthorized recycling.>

"I was just going to get in some practice," explained CD to the BOSS. "No one in their right mind could possibly want any of these selections. They're *so* dull. Unique is *in*, BOSS."

<Human assistance not currently required in music center. JDM off-limits to Y'Ad Callista Derry unless tourist requests mix.>

CD frowned. "When I was assigned to my position at Desert Depot, the C'Off told me I would be working in juke-disc production."

<Human assistance not currently required in music center. JDM off-limits to Y'Ad Callista Derry unless tourist requests mix.>

"But the C'Off assured me that I would be working in juke-disc production."

<Human assistance not currently required in music center. JDM off-limits to Y'Ad Callista Derry unless tourist requests mix.>

"Stop that!" said CD, annoyed. "The C'Off said I could use this equipment!"

<Human assistance not currently required...>

"Oh, *politicians!*" swore CD as she marched out of the music center.

After that, the day rapidly deteriorated. The souvenir center was open, and CD sat obediently behind the counter, but not one solar-bus arrived.

It was very quiet and lonely, and for the first time, a germ of rebellion began to grow in CD's mind. She knew the BOSS had no emotion and no human perspective, so she didn't blame the BOSS for her boredom, but she *was* rather put out with AusLaw. AusLaw said she had to work. Fine, she was willing to work! But the BOSS wouldn't let her use the JDM until a tourist required a mix. If there were no tourists to request anything, why was she here at all? She shrugged and sighed. AusLaw must have its reasons. Its megachip brain didn't make mistakes.

Night came suddenly to the desert, and CD went to her quarters to sleep. The familiar decor was soothing, and she could almost pretend she was home in the city. She could imagine opening the door and stepping into the next room, where her parents would be waiting.

The thought made her homesick, so she activated the vidwindow. The screen shimmered, grayed, and cleared to show the very scene she had imagined. Her parents were eating their evening rations and at first they didn't notice the call.

"Hi," said CD.

Ashlin and Willan Derry looked around and smiled.

"CD!" said Willan. "How's it going, Pr'Ad?"

"Y'Ad!" corrected CD automatically. The strangeness of the day was dissolving in the warmth of her dad's familiar grin.

"Y'Ad, of course!" said Willan, respectfully. "What's it like at Desert Depot, CD? Are all the tourists keeping you busy?"

"What tourists?"

"I thought that might be the case," said Ashlin. "Is there anyone else there?"

"There's a BOSS."

"There's always a BOSS," said Willan.

"This is a Mark-17."

"Then you should really get along quite well," said Willan. "At least the Mark-17s have got something to say for themselves."

"Yes, and they keep on saying it!" said CD. "*How* they keep on saying it!"

Her parents smiled, and they looked so close that CD felt she could almost put out a hand to tug Ashlin's braided hair. She stopped herself and blew them a kiss instead. "Y'Ad signing off!" she said cheerfully and closed down the vidwindow.

The screen fuzzed and went dark, and CD sighed. She strolled over to her window and looked out, not at the green checkerboard of the city, but at the endless flat plain of the Great Stone Desert. She peered out into the dark… and the dark peered back with golden eyes.

CD gasped and almost called out, but there was no one to hear her except for the BOSS, so she blinked instead and rubbed her eyes. When she looked again, the golden gaze was gone.

CHAPTER 4

Lone-One

CD was afraid. There were golden eyes out in the desert, and no policams to keep her safe. She could reach her parents again, but what could they do? Nothing.

CD turned off the light and peered back through the window. She could see nothing in the desert darkness. When she gazed around her room, the holo-posters shone in the moonlight. The Siamese seemed to arch its back, and the Persian seemed to sneer. CD knew it was a trick of light, just the moon reflecting the holographic images as it did in the city. But this was the desert, not the city. There was no one around to help her except for the BOSS.

Out in the desert, the sun's warmth had leaked back into the atmosphere. The thorn lizards had settled under their rocks, and the ants had filed into their anthills to wait for the sun's return. Nocturnal animals, mostly small marsupials, hopped or skittered across the arid ground, going about their business and ignoring Desert Depot just as they ignored larger rocks and piles of stone. From their perspective, Desert Depot had always been there, and had nothing to do with them. Even the dingoes, the wild dogs that wandered the desert looking for food, ignored the domes. If Desert Depot had housed sheep or fowl, the dingoes would have thought it worth a visit. Since it housed a cold metallic BOSS and a single human being, the dingoes passed it by. They didn't care for humans, and the BOSS was no more appetizing than a tin can.

Only Lone-One spared a glance at Desert Depot. Lone-One knew perfectly well that the white domes of plasticrete were not part of the natural scene. Lone-One was as wary and wild as a dingo, and very, very clever. It liked the sun and had snoozed the daylight hours away, but it had seen the young Two-Leg arrive. It had watched the creature walk into the desert, then seen it turn back to the place of domes.

Later, in the moonlight, Lone-One prowled the desert plain, the rocks and stones never rolling under its tread. An arch of yellow light shining through a window drew its attention to the place of domes. Lone-One sprang to a vantage point and peered into the place that had always been dark before. The young Two-Leg was framed in the arch of light, peering out into the desert. Lone-One froze, still and silent. Its eyes dilated, flooding its dark pupils with moonlight. The young Two-Leg was watching Lone-One, and Lone-One knew it must not be seen.

Lone-One flowed from the rock and went on its way, but later, when the arch of yellow light had darkened, Lone-One returned. Creeping close to the place of domes, it peered through the window, but there wasn't much to see. Its pupils widened to their greatest extent, but still the young Two-Leg was nothing but a shadow behind the glass.

CD slept restlessly, dreaming of cats and music.

The desert doesn't change.
Sometimes it rains
and sometimes it doesn't.
Sometimes it's hot
and sometimes it's cold.
The desert grows a little
or shrinks a little
or gets a little bit green,
but it doesn't really change.
Only people change.

CD read the words on the holo-poster for the tenth time. The holo-poster shifted from pink to green, and she read it for the eleventh time. It still didn't make sense.

"The desert's always changing, you futile fillet of polyfiber!" said CD. "How can you possibly say it stays the same?"

The holo-poster didn't answer her, and neither did anyone else.

CD looked at the calendar on the wall. She'd been at Desert Depot for two months, and she had another ten months to go before she was due to leave. Only one day stood out in her memory: the day she had accessed the breedbanks through the vidwindow and logged her order for a pet. One rex clone-kit, order 1789X. She didn't know what the "X" stood for, but hoped it was a priority. That had been six weeks ago, and she was still waiting for notification that her pet was ready to collect.

CD sighed, turned her back on the calendar, and picked up another holo-poster.

FIRST STOP –
DESERT DEPOT!
Meals, music, and merchandise
Refreshments to satisfy your taste
Juke-disc music, holo-posters
Choose a souvenir

CD pondered her position. It's supposed to be *my* job to organize refreshments, mix the music, and demonstrate the merchandise to tourists, isn't it? Wasn't that what the C'Off said at my interview?

After two months, she was increasingly unsure of what the C'Off had actually said, but she thought it was something like that. She thought he'd promised her thorn lizards and juke-disc production, but the thorn lizards remained obstinately unfriendly, and the BOSS wouldn't let her play with the JDM. It really upset CD to know all that wonderful equipment was there, just out of reach.

She thought the C'Off had also promised her tourists. What *had* she done to be banished out here?

She caught herself reading the holo-poster for the twelfth time as it shifted from blue to purple. "Stop that!" she said sternly, but again there was no reply.

CD swung around on her stool. "Hey, BOSS," she said, "why don't we stock a few oral-response holos for a change? They might prove to be a bit more interesting than this thing. Maybe someone might even want to take one home!"

<Effort ineffective.> said the BOSS.

"Effort ineffective!" exclaimed CD. "How can you know it's *effort ineffective* if you've never tried it, you rusty bucket of bolts?"

<Effort ineffective.> repeated the BOSS.

CD rolled her eyes. There was no use arguing with the BOSS. It didn't argue back, but simply repeated its original remark over and over. Her father said he liked BOSSes because they never played favorites and never made mistakes.

Her grandfather apparently agreed. He said BOSSes never took vacations or victimized workers, and they never played golf. They also never suffered from any kind of executive stress.

"No," said CD aloud. "You can leave that to me."

She wasn't sure what executive stress actually was, but her grandfather had told her it was a product of the

Days of Waste, so she supposed it was probably a bad thing to have.

"Do you have executive stress, BOSS?" she asked.

<Nonapplicable.> said the BOSS.

CD scowled at the BOSS's shiny steel blue finish and bland screen. The thing was her overseer and she was supposed to treat it with respect, but how could she respect a hunk of noncorrosive metal with a macrochip brain and five thousand preprogrammed words and phrases? She didn't need the BOSS, and she was certain the BOSS didn't need her. It could have run Desert Depot quite well on its own. It *had* run Desert Depot quite well on its own before she came. By now, *she* could have run Desert Depot, too.

"I wish you looked human," she said suddenly. "There'd be some point to you if you looked human. Then we could play cards or something when business was bad."

<Bionic Over-SeerS human structure contra-indicated.> said the BOSS.

"All right. Don't get your syntax in a twist," said CD. "Let's close up shop. I want to go for a walk in the desert that never changes."

<Desert Depot business hours are between 7:00 a.m. and 6:00 p.m. daily.> said the BOSS.

"There hasn't been a customer in nine days."

<There is no reason to believe this current state of affairs will continue.>

"Great," said CD. "And what if I want a day off to walk in the desert?"

<Leisure leave granted on grounds of necessity. You have already completed essential exercise requirement. Is your journey necessary?>

"*Yes*," said CD. "Definitely. Otherwise I might start climbing walls in here."

<Vertical ascent of interior structure not recommended.> said the BOSS.

CD laughed. Occasionally, just occasionally, the BOSS said something amusing.

"Right on, BOSS," she said, and sat down, winding her legs around the stool at the counter and turning her back on the holo-poster. "I'll behave, but I'm warning you: If something doesn't happen soon, I'll start reading that holo-poster for the thirteenth time today. After that, a vertical ascent will start looking pretty good. Why don't these holo-posters ever say anything sensible, anyway? Maybe someone would want one of them if they did. Why don't we have some cat holo-posters like the ones I brought from the city? Tourists – when there are any – would love them."

<Cats are contra-indicated in a sensitive natural desert environment.> reproved the BOSS. <Cats may turn feral. Feral animals pose unacceptable risk to wildlife. Sightings of all feral animals must be reported to AusLaw.>

"Well, I'm going to have my own cat soon," said CD. "My application has already gone through."

<Cats are contra-indicated in a sensitive natural desert environment. Cats may turn feral. Feral animals pose unacceptable risk to wildlife. Sightings of all feral animals must be reported to AusLaw.>

“*My* cat will be a pet. It won’t turn feral,” said CD.

<Cats are contra-indicated in a sensitive natural. . .>

“SHUT UP!” yelled CD at the top of her lungs. “SHUT UP, SHUT UP!”

The BOSS shut up.

Out in the desert, Lone-One pricked up its ears and fanned out its long whiskers. The young Two-Leg was making a noise.

CHAPTER 5

Encounter

CD had been very pleased to be finished with school. She could read, sing, calculate, and access data as necessary. Her formal education was officially complete. Now, with plenty of time to spare and no one other than the BOSS to keep her company, she had revised her opinion of school.

School had never been this lonely, and there was a lot she didn't know. In self-defense, she took to spending her leisure hours either fulfilling her compulsory exercise by walking in the desert or studying her data-disc. Both the data-disc and desert had plenty to teach her.

During her walks, she proved over and over again that the holo-poster had it all wrong. The desert was constantly changing. When it rained, the brown landscape would flush with green, and sometimes she would even find wildflowers. Occasionally, she encountered a thorn lizard or a battalion of ants, and sometimes a dust devil danced across the rocks like a whirling funnel. She would find odd tracks in a patch of sand or dust, and at other times she discovered cast-off feathers or the brittle bones of some small animal. And then there were the little desert hawks that rode the updrafts and looked like dark arrowheads against the hot blue sky.

CD was coming to know the desert, to read its moods, and to like it, although cautiously. Even now, it felt odd to be unmonitored, but without policams to look out for her, she had to be more observant herself.

During other spare hours, she read her data-disc, trekking back through the years to the Days of Waste, reading of crime, injustice, and rebellion.

She read of many foolish decisions, of leaders who hesitated when they might have acted, and of others who acted when it was unwise, unnecessary, or even wrong to do so.

She read about animals, discovering that cats had not always been clones and that dingoes were not native to Australia, and that there had once been large cream orange cats with dark stripes on their coats – the great lords of the cat tribe.

She read that deserts could be either natural or human-made, that stars were globes of gas, and that it had once been legal to have more than one child in a family.

She read of all the things her grandfather had told her, and these half-forgotten scraps of information began to blend into a picture of life the way it had been.

She read until her eyes ached with tiredness, then she walked out in the desert. Sometimes she talked to the BOSS and made half-hearted attempts to gain access to the JDM, or tried to interest the few customers who wandered into the souvenir center in the things it had to offer.

In two whole months she had not persuaded a single tourist to take a holo-poster home. Some tourists *did* want music, but despite her best offers to mix whalesong with vintage rock and the most modern melodiscs, no one wanted anything but copies of the premixed discs. And why should they want anything else? CD thought drearily. Tourists didn't come into the desert to buy music or posters; they came into the desert simply to experience old-time travel on a solar-bus. And most of them, having experienced it for the eight solid hours it took to reach Desert Depot, reeled from the vehicle with glazed eyes and parched throats, drank several glasses of water, sprawled out in the chairs, and wished loudly that they had taken a jet-carrier instead.

"I guess it's because they're Sen'Cits," said CD to the BOSS. "If there were some Y'Ads, I could mix some music. I could show them the desert. It would be fun."

<Y'Ads do not tour.> said the BOSS.

"They ought to," said CD. "Y'Ads would like the desert. They'd like the music. BOSS, why am I here?"

<To work.> said the BOSS.

"But there's nothing I can do. Everything here is done automatically. What have I done? Why was I sent here?"

<Humans want human staff. AusLaw demands it. Project Human Touch.> reminded the BOSS.

"But BOSS, this place is so inefficient," said CD. "It's here for the tourists, and how many have we seen? Three solar-buses and five jet-carriers in two months. And four of the jet-carriers didn't even stop. I must have done something bad to be sent to a place like this."

The BOSS just ignored her, so to avoid reading the holo-poster for the fifteenth time for that particular day, she thought about her cat.

The idea of her cat had gone from being a future pleasure to being an obsession, so real she could almost imagine she had it already. She was getting a rex, and she could hardly wait, but she *did* wish she hadn't accessed the information on the data-disc.

Cat breeds had once been many and varied, with so many colors and types and temperaments. Now, CD knew what she was missing. She would have her rex clone-kit, and that would be wonderful, but there would be no real surprises. Her rex would be exactly like every other rex in the country. In a way, it *was* every other rex in the country. Nevertheless, it would be *her* cat, and special.

Just before dark, CD closed the souvenir center and walked out into the desert, taking her evening rations to eat on the way. She sat down on a rock and hugged her knees, wishing Ashlin and Willan could see the desert. The vidwindow allowed her to talk to them every day, but it wasn't the same. She would have liked to have talked to her grandfather, too, but Galway didn't have a vidwindow. He said he preferred to do his visiting the old-fashioned way, in person. He had applied to AusLaw for a vidwindow exemption. It had been granted until he became an Eld, when he would have to have it installed for his own protection.

Now *that* was an idea! Galway was a Sen'Cit, so why shouldn't he take a solar-bus tour? He could visit her here at Desert Depot, and she could tell him all the things she had learned and show him around. Galway wasn't another Y'Ad, but he was always fun to talk to. And Galway could be convinced to choose a juke-disc mix worthy of her talents. She'd make sure of that.

CD wondered why she hadn't thought of it before. With something new to look forward to, she began to eat her rations with a renewed appetite.

Lone-One pricked up its ears and sniffed the wind. Its gold eyes blinked and its nostrils widened: food.

Lone-One sniffed again, slightly puzzled. It could not identify the substance. Not Flying-One, not Slithery-One, not even Hopping-One. Lone-One's narrow sides heaved as it sighed. Life was tough in the desert. Its litter-mates had long since gone away, most of them dead. Lone-One had remained near the place of domes. Lone-One was wily and cunning and did what it had to do to survive. Always, it looked for ways to improve its situation, but there was never quite enough food to fill its belly.

Drawn by the smell, Lone-One glided quickly from the shelter and crept on silent paws into the wind. Its whiskers twitched as it detected another smell. It was the scent of the young Two-Leg.

During the past two months, Lone-One had observed the young Two-Leg several times, though always at a distance. Its continued presence at the place of domes had made little difference, but still Lone-One remained interested. The young Two-Leg plus the food smell: the young Two-Leg either *was* food or *had* food. And food was what Lone-One wanted.

Moving in a crouch, its elbows almost higher than its sinuous back, Lone-One stalked the young Two-Leg. Lone-One could smell an abundance of food, more than it could eat in a meal or even three meals. Lone-One would have full-belly for days.

Lone-One paused, its tail twitching doubtfully. The young Two-Leg was bigger than it had thought, and Lone-One wasn't used to such large prey. Lone-One was worried it might fail to make a kill.

The young Two-Leg didn't look dangerous, but looks, as in the case of Slithery-One, could be deceiving. A Slithery-One had pierced Lone-One's paw once and Lone-One had been very ill for days. Lone-One's paw had swelled badly and Lone-One had almost followed its litter-mates into death. Since then, unless it caught one basking unawares, Lone-One left Slithery-Ones alone.

Lone-One switched its tail indecisively, and that was a mistake. The young Two-Leg had been gazing at a small flock of Flying-Ones (delicious but out of reach), but Lone-One's movement had attracted its attention. The young Two-Leg turned its strange pale face downwind, and its eyes and mouth widened in alarm. Lone-One snarled in frustration, its belly tightening with hunger. The young Two-Leg rose and began to retreat toward the place of domes as Lone-One watched in bitter disappointment.

The opportunity for days of full-belly was lost, but Lone-One resolved to try again when the opportunity presented itself. Meanwhile, though the young Two-Leg was out of reach, perhaps there was something to be learned from the place where it had rested.

The smell of food still lingered on the rock, and Lone-One was gratified to find that some of the food did, too. The substance was unfamiliar, but a cautious sniff and a taste proved it to be edible. Better yet, there were no feathers, fur, claws, or indigestible beak. It was all food, and of the very best quality.

Crouching, Lone-One ate the offering and licked its whiskers clean.

CD's heartbeat raced uncomfortably as she let herself inside Desert Depot. She had left her rations out on the rock, and she could draw no more until tomorrow, but she had no inclination to go back to search for them. Not with that *thing* out there. That *thing* was… Well, CD wasn't sure what it was, but it wasn't a native animal.

She considered using the vidwindow to contact Ashlin and Willan, but what could they do but worry? No doubt they'd remind her of her obligation to report the matter to AusLaw and tell her to remain inside Desert Depot until an investigation had been completed and the creature assessed for removal or destruction.

CD knew she should make the report immediately, but she needed to think first. Perhaps whatever it was had meant no harm. Perhaps she had misread the expression in its gold eyes. And perhaps she had imagined the whole episode.

Cats didn't come that color. Not anymore. And cats didn't come that big.

Not wanting to be alone, she went to find the BOSS. "BOSS, you know about the desert," she said. "Tell me about the animals here."

<Access promofilm.> said the BOSS.

Of course! The information she needed would be covered in the promofilms stocked in the souvenir center. But would the BOSS allow her to use one? It was fiercely protective of the JDM. She glanced doubtfully at the BOSS's screen. "May I access promofilm, BOSS?" she asked.

<Access promofilm.> repeated the BOSS.

That sounded like permission, if not a direct order, so CD picked up a promofilm and activated the switch.

The souvenir center faded and the desert appeared around her, wind, sand, rocks, and all. But it was not the desert *she* knew. The small flowers she occasionally saw were all on show, and the brilliant light was filtered to an even gold. A rainbow arched across the sky, and three small marsupials hopped into view and began nibbling brush.

A dingo appeared and sat lazily in the sun, and there were no bones, no dying plants, and no lines of marching ants. And the smell of flowers was absent. This was a desert, but not her desert. This was the desert the way the tourists would like it to be.

A soothing voice-over began to describe the wonders of the region, detailing the types of marsupials, the little hawks, and the reptiles, insects, and dingoes.

> *Wildlife is limited to a few species that are fully adapted to the harsh conditions. Days of Waste species, such as rabbits, foxes, and imported birds, have long been destroyed, and now only creatures whose right it has always been to coexist in the desert do so. Ferals have been exterminated, and the delicate balance of nature has been restored. Those touring the desert are requested to remain within their solar-buses at all times, except at registered rest stops such as Desert Depot. A local guide may offer short pedestrian tours. No naturally occurring material is to be removed from this area.*

The promofilm continued showing desert plants and animals, and CD watched it through to the end. The holograph faded and the souvenir center reappeared.

Thoughtfully, she replaced the promofilm on the shelf. It hadn't told her much, but there had been one thing that seemed unusual – the continuing existence of the dingoes.

Her data-disc had informed her that dingoes were not an original Australian species. They were in the dog family, and not marsupials, and had come from some other part of the world thousands of years before. If that was so, why did AusLaw allow them to continue to live in the desert? And if only dingoes and original species survived, what had the *thing* been?

CHAPTER 6

Research

CD stayed inside Desert Depot for the next two days. It was safe in there, but every so often she found herself cautiously opening the door or glancing nervously out of the window at the desert. In the heat of the day there were very few animals of any kind visible, but as the shadows began to lengthen, she did see two lean, sand-colored forms flit by – dingoes.

CD watched them until they were out of sight. Could it possibly have been a dingo that she had seen? It looked a little too small, and the shape was different, but she was at least willing to consider the possibility. After all, it could *not* have been a cat. The only cats that had ever been that big had been extinct for over a century and had *never* lived in Australia anyway. Besides, leopards, lions, and even tigers had never been that strong shade of orange.

A solar-bus of tourists arrived on the third day, and CD, welcoming them to Desert Depot, found herself anxiously scanning the desert beyond. What if that *thing* attacked a tourist? Native wildlife was protected, and most species were not aggressive, but the *thing* was different. It couldn't be classed as a native, and its golden gaze had held something stronger than fear.

Instead of urging the touring Sen'Cits to enjoy a stroll in the desert, as she usually did, CD steered them firmly into the souvenir center. Without waiting for them to make a request (which they probably wouldn't have made), she activated the promofilm and watched the holographic desert materialize around them. Only a few showed any interest in watching the promo. The others said they'd seen enough of the desert from the solar-bus, so CD guided them into the music center. As usual, she tried to interest them in letting her compile a personalized juke-disc, but as usual, they settled for the prerecorded programs.

The BOSS, which had been busy overseeing the rehydration of the solar-bus, trundled in soon afterward. Its appearance reminded the Sen'Cits that their vehicle was ready to depart, so they left at once.

Watched impassively by the BOSS, CD tidied the souvenir center, restocked the sample juke-discs, and then retreated to her own quarters. Rather to her surprise, the vidwindow was already activated. She peered at the screen, not at her familiar home in the city, but at an office. Behind the console sat a figure clad in the red uniform of a M'Ad. She didn't know him.

"Yes?" she said.

The M'Ad was giving her a doubtful look, as if he wondered whether he had the right person. "Y'Ad Callista Derry?"

"CD," she corrected. "Yes, that's me."

"You applied for a clone-kit. A rex, I believe?"

"Oh! Yes, yes, I did," said CD. "Is it ready?"

"Your selection is waiting at the breedbanks. You must collect it in person within seven days. With your clone-kit, you will receive a suitable supply of cat food and other requirements, an owner's manual, and a declaration form establishing your agreement to take complete care and control of your cat. Thank you."

"Oh!" CD felt her mouth curving in a smile. "Thank you!" she said, and glanced appraisingly at the pet quarters in the corner of her room. Very soon now they would be occupied by a curly coated rex. "But wait! I can't come. I'm working at Desert Depot."

"I beg your pardon?"

"I'm at Desert Depot. AusLaw sent me here weeks ago, and of course, there's no speed-rail."

The M'Ad looked at her with distaste. "Then you are clearly unable to collect your order. Shall I cancel?"

CD hesitated. She couldn't leave Desert Depot but surely she could have the cat brought to her. She thought about the possible couriers and settled on her grandfather. He could bring it when he came on the solar-bus – *if* he came on the solar-bus.

"M'Ad, is it permitted to have the collection made by someone else? A Sen'Cit, perhaps?" she asked.

"Most irregular," said the M'Ad, but he had to agree there was nothing in the rules to forbid it.

"Then please place a short-term hold on that order," she said. "I shall arrange for Sen'Cit Galway Derry to make the collection."

The M'Ad looked very annoyed. "Two months, maximum," he said, and closed the vidwindow.

Her clone-kit was ready, but what about the *thing?* CD had managed to push back her uncertainty, but her discussion with the M'Ad brought back her fears in a rush. Was the *thing* dangerous? Would it harm her pet or the tourists? She didn't know, but she was pretty sure it was already harming the local wildlife. If she was right, it was her duty to report its existence and activities to AusLaw. AusLaw would then make an assessment and exterminate the *thing.* CD bit her lip. Extermination was awfully final, even more final than deregistration.

CD reactivated the vidwindow, but as the emblem of AusLaw swam into view, she lost her courage and switched the vidwindow to her home in the city. CD hoped to speak to her parents, but the brightening screen showed an empty room. "So," CD wondered aloud. "What now?"

Of course, the *thing* might be a native species she had somehow overlooked. In that case, reporting it would be a waste of AusLaw's time. She closed the vidwindow and went to her data-disc instead. With a little luck, she might be able to identify the *thing* and find out what threat – if any – it might pose.

Quickly, CD searched the data-disc index.

"Animals" was too broad a subject, so she narrowed the parameters to "Australian Desert, Marsupials, Cats, and Mammals."

"Marsupials" yielded a very long, detailed reading list. "Nonmarsupial" was much shorter, with a simple entry on dingoes.

Frowning, CD accessed "Cats" and began to read the displayed information.

Felines – Australian Availability

There are now six breeds of *Felis domesticus* currently available as pets: Siamese, Russian blue, ragdoll, Manx, rex, and Persian. Animated identification holo-displays follow.

CD skipped over the holo-displays. She already had the reproductions on her walls. She skipped the characteristics of each breed as well, and backtracked to the history section.

Domestic Cats

18th century: Cats arrive in Australia with European settlers.

19th century: Feral cats begin to become a problem for local wildlife.

20th century: Feral cat problem recognized. Minor extermination carried out.

21st century: Sterilization and licensing required for all domestic cats. Breeding stock exempted. Clone-kits program initiated. Exemptions terminated.

22nd century: Australian clone-kits program expanded. Ferals eliminated by the widening availability of sterile clone species.

Current century: See "Felines - Australian Availability."

CD studied the clone-kits program and widened the topic to include selective breeding. That was where she found the first clue.

Selective Breeding

In selective breeding (clone-kits, etc.), the best, most docile, representatives of a particular breed are chosen for breeding or cloning desirable qualities.

Natural Selection

In natural selection (survival of the fittest), the effect is different. The biggest, strongest examples of a breed fight off predators and get more to eat. They survive to breed, and each generation, instead of remaining docile as in selective breeding, grow larger and less manageable. See also "Desert-Feral."

CD initiated the search, and suddenly, right in front of her, there it was.

Desert-Feral

A desert-feral is a semi-mythical example of natural selection. During the 21st century, some feral cats retreated to the desert where, by means of natural selection, they became larger than their ancestors. Unsubstantiated reports of desert-ferals (dubbed *Felis australis*) massing some fifty kilograms were recorded, but the largest specimen ever trapped was some twenty kilograms lighter. Desert-ferals were eradicated and have been extinct since the turn of the century.

"Oh, have they!" said CD aloud. "Have they really!"

So the *thing* was a *cat*-thing. CD was relieved to have identified it. The thought of a savage feral animal out there was not very pleasant, but it was much better than letting her imagination go completely wild. So the cat-thing was a desert-feral – *Felis australis*. It originated and was then *supposedly* eradicated in less than two centuries!

Now she must report her discovery to AusLaw. A feral animal at large in the desert would be a disaster! She shuddered to think how many marsupials, birds, and reptiles the cat-thing must have killed already. And yet, desert-ferals were extinct. So what if the cat-thing wasn't a desert-feral after all?

Data-disc research was all very well, but sometimes one had to know more.

CHAPTER 7

Oasis

CD thought about her dilemma for some time. Several times she opened the vidwindow to make her report, but just as often she closed it again. The desert-feral (if it was *truly* a desert-feral) could not be allowed to remain in the desert, but she hated to be the one to cause its removal and destruction. If it was so very rare (could it be the only one?), it was almost certainly an endangered species.

There was a good chance that her report would be totally unnecessary, of course. The BOSS had probably alerted AusLaw to the presence of the cat-thing long ago. But if it had, why had AusLaw not acted? Could it possibly be waiting to see if *she* would do her duty?

CD shivered. Most of the things AusLaw did were incomprehensible to a mere Y'Ad like herself. AusLaw had a Mark-5000 megachip brain, while her brain was only tissue and synapses.

She sat at the window for several hours, straining her eyes and worrying. Occasionally, she would shiver again, feeling herself watched. Surveillance by policams had been a way of life in the city, but this was entirely different. Watcher and watched – CD wasn't sure she liked being both and thought perhaps the desert-feral didn't like it either.

After a time, she turned out her light and continued to gaze out over the desert plain while her eyes became accustomed to the moonlight. Strange, how the tawny desert became gray and black at night. The sand-colored dingoes were dark shadows, and the little marsupials looked like shadow puppets against the sky. A large rock cast a pool of darkness… Surely there was no rock in that location! She would have noticed it before. Puzzled, CD leaned forward.

As she watched, the "rock" drew itself up and padded forward. Unmistakably, its head turned, and she saw the flash of golden alien light – cat's eyes!

CD gasped. The desert-feral had been observing her, all right – watcher and watched.

It stood there for a few seconds, then slowly padded closer to the window. CD shrank back. The glass was thick and she was safe, but it was very unnerving to see the cat-thing so close.

It came right up to the window, pressing its soft, heavy forepaws, almost the size of CD's own palms, against the glass. She could see the long claws in the moonlight; the fine hairs that radiated from the square, flat face; the broad, half-flattened ears; and the faint mist of breath on the pane. It was obviously a cat. A giant cat.

Nervously, she licked her lips and stepped back. Perhaps the movement alarmed the creature, or perhaps it had simply finished its inspection, for it removed its paws from the glass and dropped to all fours. It padded away slowly, blending with the rocks and brush until CD could not tell where it had gone.

The young Two-Leg was still at the place of domes. It no longer came out to roam the desert, but it was still there. Lone-One wondered about that. Potential prey often became wary, but if the young Two-Leg was afraid, why did it sit visibly behind the barrier? Why didn't it hide away in the depths of the place of domes?

Lone-One made a close inspection later in the night, but not only did the cold, clear barrier take away touch, it also took away smell, and Lone-One could learn little that it did not already know.

Lone-One would be patient, but not for very long. Lone-one had to find out. It had to *know*.

The next day, CD ventured outside the dome of Desert Depot for the first time in three days. She really had no excuse for any further investigations, for it was obvious that her eyes were right and the data-disc was wrong. Desert-ferals were *not* extinct, but this one soon would be if she notified AusLaw.

CD took her morning ration and laid it safely on a rock while she searched the area beyond her window for prints. She found none on the ground – the rocky terrain made a poor surface for prints. Almost absently, CD began to clear some of the rocks away from the place directly below the window. There was dry, reddish soil underneath. She wondered if anything but brush would ever grow here. Of course there were always the wildflowers that sprang up after a rain, but they were few and far between, and they didn't last long. Soon her fingertips began to hurt, so she left her self-imposed task and looked closely at the window itself.

There, on the glass, were the prints she had not found on the ground. A little smudged, but undeniably cat's paws. There was even a small, round spot, as if a cat had bumped the glass with its nose.

The back of CD's neck began to prickle, and she raised her hand to rub it. The sensation persisted. From the corner of her eye, she was aware of a sudden movement, slight as a cloud's shadow, and quick as a darting thorn lizard. She glanced around, but there was nothing to see.

Not even her morning ration.

"Politicians!" complained CD. Something had stolen her morning ration, taken it neatly and wholly from the rock – the desert-feral!

"All right," said CD softly. "If that's the way you want it! At least you didn't try taking *me*." She shivered, thinking how close the creature must have been.

CD sucked her upper lip, a habit she had when thinking hard. The desert-feral had come close, but it had not harmed her. It had eaten synthetic protein instead. CD played around with the idea of making a report, but instead began to whistle softly. The sun grew stronger, and a haze of heat began to close in over the desert as she went back into the dome.

She'd see the desert-feral again, CD promised herself. And this time, it wouldn't be through a barrier of glass. Disobedience was beginning to get easier.

The BOSS was waiting for her in the souvenir center. "Hi!" said CD.

<Desert Depot business hours are between 7:00 a.m. and 6:00 p.m. daily.> said the BOSS.

"I know," said CD. "There are no tourists today."

<Desert Depot business hours are between 7:00 a.m. and 6:00 p.m. daily.>

"I *know!*" said CD. "There's nothing for me to do in here when there are no solar-buses. *Listen,* BOSS, I have an idea."

<Desert Depot business hours. . .>

"This is *for* the business. It's for the tourists," said CD. "It would be good if the tourists stayed here longer, wouldn't it BOSS?"

<Average length of tourist stay now thirty minutes.> said the BOSS.

Its voice was mechanical, but to CD the BOSS sounded a bit sad.

"Boss," said CD, "about the desert-feral. Have you reported it to AusLaw?"

<Desert-feral is a semi-mythical creature. Extinct.> Without a pause, the BOSS then reverted to the subject it really wanted to discuss. <Average length of tourist stay now thirty minutes.> it repeated, almost sorrowfully.

"Perhaps we just need another attraction." CD was feeling her way, knowing that if she asked outright for time to spend observing the desert-feral, the BOSS would refuse and remind her of her obligations to AusLaw. "If we had another attraction," she coaxed, "the average length of a stay might be an hour, or even more! If only we could make the place more interesting and attractive to Sen'Cits."

The BOSS said nothing, but CD had the distinct feeling that it was waiting for her to say more. "All the people who come here say they have seen enough of the desert," she said. "They don't know it the way we do, and they don't like it. If we made the *outside* of Desert Depot a bit more attractive, perhaps they would want to stay awhile and rest their eyes."

<How?> said the BOSS.

"We could have an outside garden. If we cleared some of the rocks and used some of the water in the big rehydrating station to make the flowers grow, it would look much better. The Sen'Cits would want to stay awhile, then."

<Liquid in rehydrating station is for use only by tourist solar-buses.> reminded the BOSS.

"Yes, but there's more than enough to rehydrate fifty solar-buses a day. We never have anything like that number. And if we used the water to make a garden, it would still be used for the tourists. Don't you think a garden would be good? Of course, it would be a lot of work outside, and AusLaw might not like it if we changed the environment."

<Oasis site.> said the BOSS.

"Huh?"

<Oasis site.>

The BOSS's habit of repeating key phrases was infuriating, but CD had learned to vary her questions to find out exactly what the BOSS did mean.

"Do you mean this would make a good oasis site?" she asked cautiously.

<Oasis site.>

"Do you mean this *is* an oasis site? Or it *was* an oasis site?"

<Correct.> confirmed the BOSS.

"I see!" And she did, now. She only wondered why she hadn't seen before.

The place where Desert Depot had been built had once been a natural oasis. It was obvious, really, that the water in the rehydrating station had to come from *somewhere.* There was no nearby river, and rain was rare, so there must be an underground supply, pumped and piped to fill the tanks.

"In that case," said CD firmly, "it is only right to return some of that water to the desert."

The BOSS was silent.

"Er, excessive storage of water is contra-indicated in a sensitive natural desert environment. Right, BOSS?"

<Correct.> said the BOSS.

There was one thing CD really liked about the BOSS. Once it had made up its macrochip brain about something, it acted right away. Within hours it had diverted a pipeline from the rehydrating station and directed CD to set up an irrigation system around the front of Desert Depot. The BOSS was not very well suited to the manual labor of removing rocks, so that job fell to CD, too.

Well, she'd wanted something to do, but as she raked and shoveled away the rocks, CD wished she'd kept her mouth shut. "It really doesn't look very fertile," she said doubtfully. "Is there anything we can do?"

The BOSS diverted some organic nutrients from the recycling plant in the hydroponics garden and added them to the desert soil.

"What about AusLaw?" asked CD.

The BOSS was very slow to answer, as it searched its vocabulary chips for an appropriate response. None fit exactly, so the BOSS assembled two or three phrases to construct an answer. <AusLaw approval. AusLaw sending suitable clone-stock plants.> it said finally.

The stock arrived the next day by jet-carrier, and for several days CD was kept very busy planting small, defenseless-looking bits of greenery and helping the BOSS set up a temporary awning to protect the fledgling garden from the desert sun.

The construction of the oasis proceeded swiftly, and was so interesting (and exhausting) that CD almost forgot that the original purpose of the oasis had been to give her an excuse to spend a great deal of time outside. She felt a little guilty at deceiving the BOSS, but after all, the BOSS didn't believe desert-ferals existed. It had said so repeatedly.

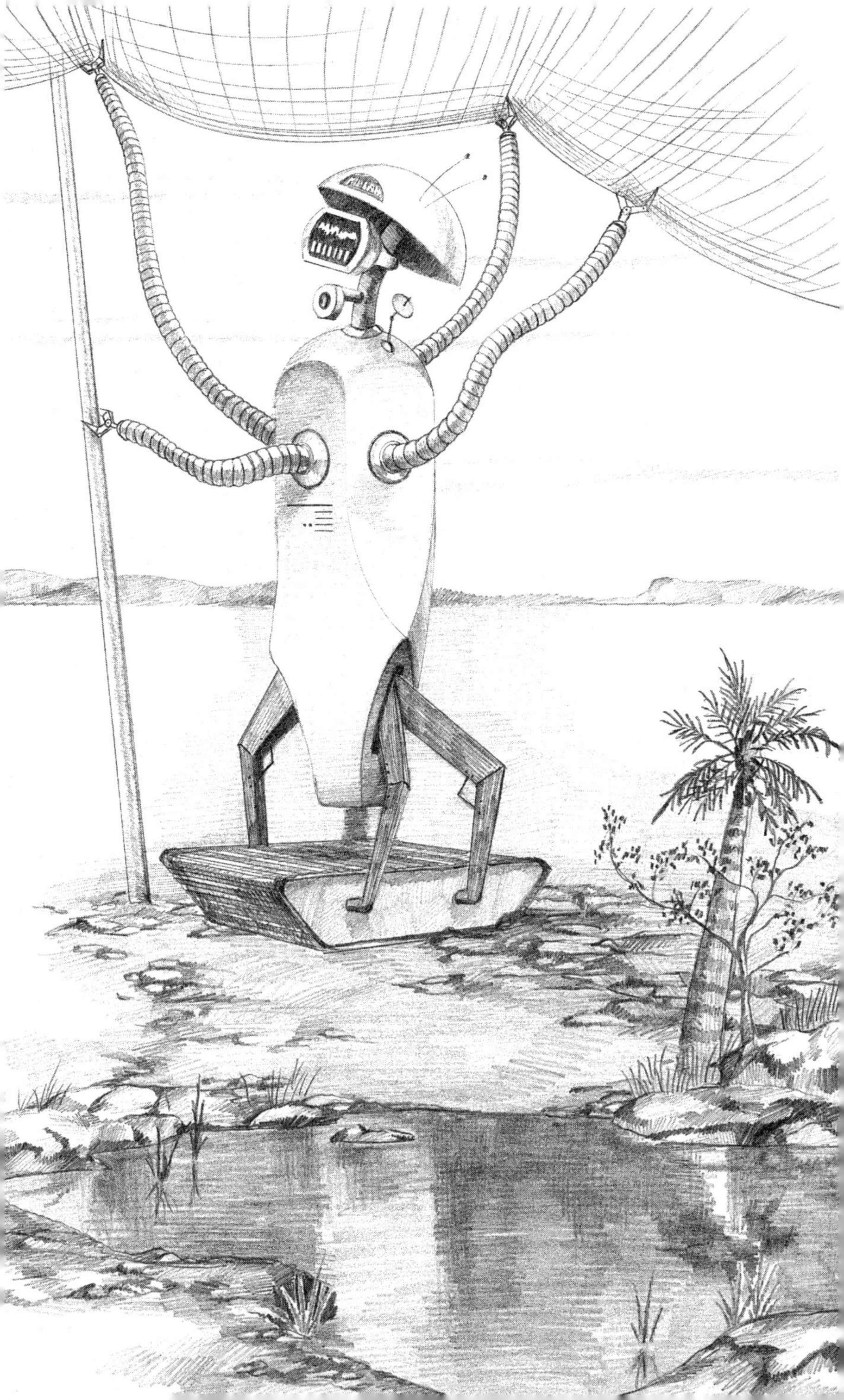

CHAPTER 8

Sen'Cit

Lone-One was very interested in the rapid growth of the place of water. Lone-One approved of a ready source of thirst-quench, and it liked the soft, cool earth. The fact that the soft earth was so close to the thirst-quench was a minor problem. Lone-One did not like to leave prints.

At first, Lone-One visited the place of water only at night. During the day the shade was tempting, but the young Two-Leg was nearly always there. Sometimes Cold-One was there, too. The scent of Cold-One was strange, sharp, inedible. The scent of the young Two-Leg was warm. Lone-One had almost given up ideas of using the young Two-Leg for full-belly, for it had begun to see that the young Two-Leg had more uses alive than dead.

It was the young Two-Leg who dug the soil and made it soft, who left food on rocks, and who had brought the thirst-quench to this place. Lone-One hoped the young Two-Leg might have other plans for Lone-One's comfort. And so it watched. And while it watched, it groomed itself, meticulously cleaning its back, chest, tail, and each paw and limb, pausing now and again to spit out the loose hairs that collected on its tongue.

As time went on, CD was more often aware that she was being watched. She sometimes glanced up from her work in the oasis to see a flicker of movement, the twitch of a long, orange tail, or sometimes she saw a gliding shadow, or gold eyes in the night.

The first time CD saw the desert-feral clearly was at sunrise, when she had ventured out to check on a few of the ailing plants. The BOSS was practical. It insisted that any plant that failed to thrive should be removed from the oasis, but CD cherished them all. She still loved the desert, but she loved the oasis, too, because she had made it. It was very small, but already she was making plans for extensions.

Sometimes, she caught herself looking forward to the time when the oasis would be large and fully developed, but that lay many years in the future. By then, she would be a M'Ad, and assigned to quite another job. She could be a Policam-Assistant perhaps, like Willan. Or a city Garden-Observer, like Ashlin. She wondered what Ashlin would think of the oasis. It was strange to think that, in these past few weeks, CD had done more actual gardening than Ashlin had done in an entire decade as a Garden-Observer.

As CD pressed the soil more firmly around the weak root system of the plant, she felt the familiar prickle on her back. Very slowly, she turned around, squinting in the sun's rising brilliance. There, poised on the rock where she often left some rations, was the desert-feral.

In the morning sunlight, the desert-feral was a strong orange color, banded with pale stripes. It had long white whiskers, broad ears, and a pinkish nose. Its eyes, slitted in the increasing light, were golden and black, and its expression was wary.

"Hello," said CD very quietly. She gazed at it, trying to decide which breed it could possibly have sprung from. There was no suggestion of Siamese coloring or the curly coat of a rex, and the aggressively restless tail showed it was no Manx. The coat was too short to make it a Persian, and its color was completely wrong for a Russian blue. It couldn't be a ragdoll, not with that arrogant stance. No, decided CD, the desert-feral wasn't a clone-kit. It was a *cat,* and that was another matter. "Hello, Cat," CD said again, and this time it sounded right and good.

Cat didn't stay long. CD made a cautious move toward it, and it snarled and bounded away. But CD had made progress, of a sort. And it was the kind of progress she knew quite well she should *not* have made.

The next time Cat appeared, CD and the BOSS were working in the oasis. The desert-feral leapt onto a rock and watched them for a long time. CD stiffened and glanced at the BOSS, but the BOSS continued with its occupation and said nothing. Neither did CD.

It was strangely timeless at Desert Depot. The Sen'Cits and solar-buses still came infrequently, but CD was gratified to realize (and to point out to the BOSS) that the touring Sen'Cits did stay a little longer, apparently intrigued by the notion of a Y'Ad doing actual manual labor.

"Why didn't AusLaw assign a BOSS capable of digging?" asked one Sen'Cit. He was a critical-looking person, and CD, whose back was aching that day, found it difficult to be polite.

"I really don't know," she said. "But I'm very glad they didn't."

The Sen'Cit snorted. "That Mark-17 is way past its prime. AusLaw should replace it."

"I like this BOSS," said CD and realized, rather to her surprise, that it was true. "It knows what to do, and it does what it can. It tells me how to do the rest."

"Extraordinary!" said the Sen'Cit. "It is incapable of human thoughts and emotions, you know."

CD smiled. “Is it?” she said.

The Sen’Cit frowned as he looked around. “Do you have a permit for this?” he asked, indicating the oasis.

“Oh, yes,” said CD. “The BOSS applied, and AusLaw granted it immediately. AusLaw even sent us the clone-stock plants to get us started.”

“Extraordinary!” said the Sen’Cit. “AusLaw must be getting soft. Granting permits for wanton vandalism on this scale!”

“Vandalism?” said CD uncertainly. “Doesn’t that mean destroying or disfiguring something, Sen’Cit?”

“Exactly.”

“But BOSS and I have created something here.”

“You have disfigured the desert.”

“No,” said CD gently but firmly. “We have simply re-created something that was here long ago. Are you also opposed to the replanting of trees and the restoration of watercourses, Sen’Cit?”

The Sen’Cit grunted, prodding the soft soil with a stick. “What’s this?” he asked abruptly.

CD looked down at the place he indicated. “Paw prints,” she said. “There’s quite a lot of native wildlife around here, Sen’Cit, and most of it likes to come to the oasis to drink.”

“Dingoes, I suppose?” said the Sen’Cit.

“There are dingoes here,” said CD. She didn’t like the way the Sen’Cit was staring at the prints, so she set out to distract him. “Now that you’ve seen the oasis, Sen’Cit, may I interest you in a holo-poster or a juke-disc?”

“These prints show no claws,” said the Sen’Cit.

"That's not so very strange," said CD firmly. "Dingoes *do* have claws, but perhaps they don't always show up in prints."

"It doesn't look like a dingo print," said the Sen'Cit. "It looks like a cat print."

CD forced herself to laugh. "Cats aren't that big, Sen'Cit! Uhm, are they?"

The Sen'Cit prodded the ground again. "Of course, you have reported this phenomenon to AusLaw, have you not, Y'Ad?"

"Reported dingo prints?" said CD. "Surely that's not necessary." She gulped, and added truthfully. "I know dingoes aren't strictly Australian animals, Sen'Cit, but I *did* check my data-disc. According to it, dingoes now are accepted as a newly evolved species. I think the reasoning is that they are so far removed from the original stock that they can't be classed as, well, feral dogs, for instance. It would be wrong to waste AusLaw's time on such a trivial matter."

"Hmm," said the Sen'Cit, "so in your informed opinion, Y'Ad, these are dingo prints?"

"What else could they be?" asked CD. "Would you care to see the holo-posters, Sen'Cit? And we have some excellent promofilm showing the wildlife in the area. You could see dingoes in action."

The Sen'Cit shook his head and continued to prowl the oasis, bending low and examining plants and rocks. For someone who disapproved of the oasis so much, he was certainly subjecting it to a thorough inspection. CD hated to leave him unattended, but by now some of the other tourists were getting restless, so she had to take them to the refreshment center and then lead them on to the souvenir center.

When the frowning, sour-faced Sen'Cit arrived at the souvenir center a short while after everyone else, his sourness seemed to have lifted a little, and CD wondered why. However, it returned in force as he inspected the center's holo-posters and the promofilm.

"Would you like one, Sen'Cit?" she asked politely.

He actually shuddered. "The desert is bad enough. I don't wish to be reminded of it at home," he said. "But I might take some music to while away the rest of this dreadful tour."

"I'll mix you a disc to your own specifications," offered CD.

"No, thank you. But I'll take a copy of one of those sample discs. The hushmusic, I think."

CD sighed, and stamped out a hushmusic disc.

"I need a small envelope to protect this," said the Sen'Cit fussily, so CD gave him one and watched uneasily as he inserted the disc. There was something odd about this man. He had hardly sampled the disc at all, and she was fairly certain he had put something else in the envelope, but it was no business of hers if he wanted another souvenir. It would have been courteous if he had asked for it, but after all, the souvenir items were there for the tourists.

The tour party stayed at Desert Depot for a record two hours and twenty minutes. CD tried to smile and act pleased for the BOSS's sake, but she was worried that the desert-feral would put in an appearance and that one of the Sen'Cits, especially the sour-faced one, would see it. If so, one of them was bound to report it, and then not only would *she* be in trouble for failing to make a report herself, but Cat would be in trouble, too. No, Cat would be *dead*.

CD attempted to look on the bright side. Unless Cat actually appeared, there was not much danger. The sour, fussy Sen'Cit had seemed very interested in the paw prints at the edge of the oasis, but they had been faint, and they really could have been made by a dingo. If *she* appeared doubtful about their origin, especially after spending so long in the desert, how could the Sen'Cit know any better?

"BOSS, what should we do about the desert-feral?" she asked when the solar-bus had finally gone.

<Desert-feral is a semi-mythical creature. Extinct.> said the BOSS.

"But they're *not* extinct," said CD. "At least this one isn't. You've seen it, BOSS – that big animal, a carnivore, that sometimes sits on the rock and watches us."

<Dingo.> said the BOSS.

"It's not a dingo."

<A desert carnivore is a dingo.> said the BOSS.

"It's a desert-feral, a giant cat."

<There are no cats present in the desert.> said the BOSS. <Cats are contra-indicated in a sensitive natural desert environment. Cats may turn feral. Feral animals pose unacceptable risk to wildlife.>

"Then why haven't you reported it?"

<Dingo is a native species. No report is necessary.>

"Nonsense," said CD. "Dingoes are as foreign as, well, cats. Or they were once."

<Dingo adapted and evolved into new species.> said the BOSS. <Allowable under AusLaw.>

CD rolled her eyes and gave up. As far as the BOSS was concerned, Cat could not be a desert-feral, because desert-ferals were supposed to be extinct. It could not be a cat, because it was too big and the wrong color. It was a large desert carnivore; therefore, it had to be a dingo.

The reasoning behind this logic seemed very strange, but after all, the BOSS was a BOSS. It could only work with the facts that were programmed into its macrochip brain. It was only a Mark-17.

But the sour-faced Sen'Cit had a human brain and human suspicions. CD didn't think he would really report his suspicions to AusLaw, but what if he told his friends about the print he had seen? Someone might come to investigate, and if that happened, it would be the end of the line for Cat. It might be the end of the line for CD, too. For her own protection, she should make a report now. CD knew that, but she could think of reasons to keep quiet, too.

She was now feeding Cat a good part of her own rations each day, in the hope that while the desert-feral had plenty of synthetic protein to eat, it wouldn't bother with the live proteins out in the desert.

So Cat's continued existence actually was doing very little harm to anyone. And that meant there might not be so *very* much trouble when – no, *if* – AusLaw finally learned of its existence.

And that meant *her* logic was just as strange as anything the BOSS might invent.

Once the oasis was planted, CD had time to think again of her pet, as well as her grandfather. The hold on her rex order was almost up, but with Cat and the oasis and the sour-faced Sen'Cit, CD had been too busy to make the required arrangements. But now, the time had come.

Early that same evening, CD used the vidwindow to contact her parents.

"Callista!" Her mother sounded surprised and pleased. "We haven't heard from you for days!"

"I've been busy," said CD.

"Really?" said Ashlin doubtfully.

"Really!" CD nodded. "Mom, it's surprising what you can do if you really try, but today the weather isn't so great, so I have a little time to spare. Listen, Mom, I need to talk to Grandad. Do you think he'd come to your quarters tomorrow?"

"I think so," said Ashlin. "Especially if I tell him it's a special request from his favorite Y'Ad."

"You do that, Mom. Thanks!" said CD. She blew Ashlin a kiss and switched off. It was time to eat, and she was very hungry. No wonder, with Cat to feed as well as herself!

CD divided her ration in half and left one part out on the usual rock. The giant cat scarcely waited for her to retreat before it came to enjoy the food. It didn't seem grateful, exactly, but it did seem hungry. Before it began to eat, it looked at her for a moment with its golden eyes, almost as if she were a friend. CD smiled back, then glanced at the sky. The clouds were gathering and the usual dry heat was humid and gray. The weather was going to change. She sighed. The oasis and the desert would benefit from rain, but she would be forced to take her exercise inside the domes.

"I wonder what *you* do when it rains," she said to Cat, but of course the desert-feral didn't answer. It simply swallowed the last of the food, polished its whiskers, and paced away into the gathering twilight.

CHAPTER 9

Rain

The next evening, as CD had hoped, Galway Derry put aside his prejudices and made a call through the vidwindow. She was surprised at how good it was to see him again, and found herself grinning widely.

Her grandfather grinned back at her, his broad face creasing in wrinkles. He was sixty-three and liked to claim a wrinkle for each year of his life. His hair was receding, but what he did have was the same color as CD's, mixed with gray. "Callie!" Galway was the only one who called her that. "Is that *rain* I hear?"

"It's pouring!" she said. "It has been all day, and it looks as if it will keep it up."

"Extraordinary!" said Galway. "But how do you like the desert?"

"Very much, now," she said, "although for a while there I was wondering what AusLaw had against me. I asked for music and animals, and what did I get? A JDM the BOSS won't let me use and a few thorn lizards and dingoes! But then, AusLaw is a Mark-5000, so you can't expect it to understand Y'Ads."

"A Mark-5000 is a little beyond human capability, certainly," mused Galway. "Or maybe a bit below it. But you say you like it now?"

"Oh yes. I've made an oasis."

"So I hear."

CD's gaze sharpened. "AusLaw licensed it, you know. This was an oasis site originally. But who told you about it?"

"I have my contacts," said her grandfather. "Among others, a certain Sen'Cit by the name of Sten Hale. Not my favorite person, but a great fund of information, mostly about things of which he disapproves. He tells me there is quite a lot of wildlife in your area."

"Yes," said CD uneasily. "There is. Listen, Grandad, you're a Sen'Cit now."

"I have been a Sen'Cit for three years. Did you have to remind me?"

"Sorry," said CD. "But since you *are* a Sen'Cit, why don't you take a solar-bus tour? That's what Sen'Cits do, you know."

"Because I don't *want* to take a solar-bus tour," said Galway. "Solar-buses are hot, dry, and dusty. Or, if the weather stays the way it is today, they are cold, damp, and muddy. And if it rains for more than twenty-four hours, the batteries can't recharge and they don't run at all. Why would I want to ride in one of those?"

"To visit me?" suggested CD.

"Hmm."

"To see my oasis?"

"Hmm."

"To order a personalized juke-disc and tell your friends about it so they'll want one, too?"

"Hmm."

"And," said CD, "to deliver my rex clone-kit. That's very important. I can't come to the city to collect it, and I need it to be delivered soon. My extension time is almost up. Please, Grandad? And don't say 'hmm' again. You're as bad as the BOSS."

"All right," said Galway. "I'll come. But I won't come in a solar-bus. I'll come by jet-carrier."

"Yes you *will* come in a solar-bus," said CD patiently. "Jet-carriers hurt your ears, so imagine what they'd do to a clone-kit!"

Galway rolled his eyes. "Then you may expect me on the next solar-bus tour, complete with clone-kit, if it is ready. Do you have the order number?"

CD gave it to him, raising her voice to be heard over the sudden increase in the deluge of rain, and Galway nodded. "Good-bye, Callie. Sen'Cit out."

Lone-One was not pleased with the rain. It hated the mud and the cold. It rained so rarely in the desert that Lone-One sometimes managed to forget that rain existed, until it came again. And now the rain had come, and Lone-One was very cold and hungry. The sunlight it loved was not available; the basking rocks were cold and dank. Lone-One wanted comfort, and as far as it could see, there was just one source of comfort in the whole streaming wet desert – the young Two-Leg.

The place of water was deserted today, so the young Two-Leg must be in the place of domes, where it was warm and dry. The young Two-Leg shared thirst-quench and food, so perhaps it would also be willing to share a dome. Lone-One went to see.

After she had finished talking to her grandfather, CD had intended to spend some time reading her data-disc, but a flicker of movement distracted her from the terminal. She glanced at the streaming window, and there was Cat, gazing at her through the glass.

CD knew the desert-feral was wet and obviously cold, but she was still worried whether it had a right to be here in the desert. It wasn't a dingo, whatever the BOSS said. And she knew she had no right to make Cat her friend. If she ignored it, the desert-feral might go away, and she would not be responsible for it anymore. Still, Cat looked so very cold.

Slowly, CD opened the window. The desert-feral bunched itself together, but instead of fleeing, it simply watched as CD picked up a small piece of synthetic protein and offered it on her palm. The gold eyes moved a little and the muzzle lifted. The desert-feral took a step forward, and then another. Water dripped from its ears and whiskers, and it flicked them irritably. CD moved back from the flying droplets, then, incredibly, the desert-feral gathered itself and sprang.

CD gasped and stumbled back, but Cat wasn't attacking. The desert-feral had simply launched itself through the window and was now crouching on the floor. There was a faint stir of warm air as the humidity controls reacted to the presence of a large, damp object. The desert-feral flicked its whiskers again and sneezed twice. It watched CD warily and sniffed. After a few moments, CD realized what it wanted, and offered the piece of synthetic protein.

Cat took it delicately from her hand, then retreated a little and ate its prize. When it was finished eating, the desert-feral began to groom the water from its coat with long sweeps of its tongue. As its fur began to dry, a hoarse, rasping sound began to percolate through the room. Surprised, CD smiled.

Cat was purring.

The desert feral spent the night curled up in a giant orange ball on the warm floor, but was gone by morning, leaving a few smudges of mud and some tufts of fur as the only reminder of its presence. CD wondered if she had imagined the episode, but that evening, when the rains closed in again, the desert-feral arrived at the window and indicated that it would like to come in.

The rain continued fitfully over the next week, and Cat took to spending a considerable amount of time in CD's quarters. The desert-feral established a comfortable roost on the padded lid of CD's clothes chest, and CD would often come in to find it already settled there, its striped paws folded demurely under its chest, its long, banded tail wrapped around its body like a scarf. Only the slight twitch of the tip of its tail and the flattening of its ears indicated that the desert-feral was not quite so relaxed as it appeared.

As for CD, she was not relaxed at all. Part of her rejoiced at this growing companionship, but the other part was afraid. Not only would AusLaw be extremely angry to find her actively harboring a feral animal, but there was also her rex clone-kit to consider. How could she possibly keep it safe while Cat claimed a share of her quarters?

She tried to shut the desert-feral out, but it was too late. Though the rain clouds cleared, and the desert steamed and dried and returned to its normal self, Cat didn't seem at all inclined to give up such a cozy bed. CD might shut the window, but she could not shut out the face pressed against the glass or the angry yowls with which the desert-feral demanded admittance. But CD also couldn't shut out the terrible fear of what would happen when her clone-kit arrived. She would have tried to apply for another extension, but she couldn't think of an excuse. Besides, Galway might already be on his way.

CHAPTER 10

JDM

The next solar-bus did not arrive for some days, but when it did lumber into sight, Galway Derry was aboard. CD had meant to be dignified, but it was such a relief to see her grandfather's familiar, kind face that she rushed to hug him. "Where is it, Grandad?" she asked. She smiled an automatic welcome to the other Sen'Cits, then suggested that they might like some refreshment.

Usually, she invited tourists to walk in the oasis first, but now she was afraid Cat would decide to investigate the crowd. She would have shut it in her quarters that morning if she'd known the solar-bus was coming. But then, Cat would probably have yowled if she had.

Galway's smile faded. "I'm sorry, Callie, but I couldn't collect your clone-kit after all."

"Oh, but…" CD swallowed her dismay and directed the other Sen'Cits into the complex. "Why, Grandad? The breedbanks won't keep it for me much longer."

"Your hold had already been terminated. Demand outweighed supply for this batch, and the breedbank's BOSS decided to let the clone-kit go to a Y'Ad who was ready to take immediate delivery." He looked a little stern. "Come on, Callie, you can't expect AusLaw to wait on *your* convenience."

"I don't," said CD. She was very disappointed, but also felt a small wave of relief. At least there would be no unpleasant confrontations between the rex clone-kit and Cat. "Another bad mark on my record," she added sadly.

Her grandfather quirked his eyebrow. "*Another* bad mark, Callie? Explain yourself."

CD shrugged. "I have to welcome these tourists. Just one moment." Summoning a smile, she showed the Sen'Cits into the refreshment area.

One Sen'Cit lingered, and she moved forward to usher him onward. "Perhaps I could interest you in the music center…" she said.

"I doubt it. You couldn't before."

CD's smile died abruptly as she recognized the Sen'Cit who had shown such interest in the prints in the oasis. He still looked just the same – his face sour but intelligent above his blue uniform.

Before she could say anything else, her grandfather cleared his throat. "*I'd* like a juke-disc," he said. "Come on, Sten, you don't know what you're missing."

So the disagreeable Sen'Cit was Sten Hale. CD wondered why he had come back. Stepping past him, CD led the way to the JDM and began to scroll the selections. Her delight at finally getting to use the equipment was soured by the nasty suspicion that Sen'Cit Sten Hale meant trouble. Her hand shook with dread, and she jumped when the BOSS trundled in.

<Human assistance not currently required in music center. JDM off-limits to Y'Ad Callista Derry unless tourist requests mix.> said the BOSS.

CD sighed. "BOSS, this tourist *has* requested a mixed disc. Isn't that right, Sen'Cit?"

"Quite right," said Galway.

<You are?>

"Galway Derry. Sen'Cit, A'L."

Galway leaned forward so the BOSS could scan his retinal print.

<You require mixed juke-disc, Galway Derry?> Somehow, the BOSS managed to inject a note of surprise into its flat, mechanical tones.

"Yes, I require a mixed juke-disc," confirmed Galway. "This center can furnish one, I trust?"

<Certainly.> said the BOSS.

"Then am I authorized to use the JDM, BOSS?" asked CD.

<Authorized.> confirmed the BOSS.

CD's spirits lifted, and she began to scroll through the choices again. "There are ten thousand selections," she told her grandfather. "Which parameters would you like me to set? And what did you mean, A'L? Is that some kind of new category, or have you done something really awful, too?"

Galway, whose interest in music was minimal, blinked at the flashing lights on the JDM. "Make a mix to your own taste, Callie, and explain what you meant by 'another bad mark' on your record."

"I thought there must have been one, for AusLaw to send me out here," said CD cautiously.

"Not at all," said Galway. "If you had a bad mark on your record, you would have been selected for a job that

kept you right under AusLaw's nose. Anyone AusLaw suspects could be a disruptive influence is kept well within range of the policams and sleepygas, Callie, not sent out to get into mischief in the desert."

CD selected whalesong and paired it deftly with some vintage classical in the same key signature. "There are no policams here," she said after a moment.

"No."

"So nothing I've done in the past three or four months has been monitored."

"I wouldn't say that."

CD's hands shook a little as she selected two more tracks. "The BOSS?" she said, trying to sound casual.

"Does the BOSS monitor me?" If it was only the BOSS, she had nothing to fear. The BOSS was her friend, and it didn't believe in desert-ferals.

"I didn't say you *were* being monitored," said Galway. "I simply suggested that you couldn't be sure. But why all the interest, Callie? Are you afraid to act without a policam to hold your hand?"

"Of course not," she said.

"And you have no reason to be afraid if someone *was* watching," said Galway. "There's a limit to the number of aggressive acts one Y'Ad can carry out in a place like this. Unless you've discovered a sudden yearning to start mugging Sen'Cits?"

CD shook her head and smiled slightly. "Only that Sten Hale. I wouldn't mind mugging him."

"But you wouldn't."

"No, of course not. That would be against AusLaw."

"Remember that, and you have nothing to worry about," said Galway. "There is no bad mark on your record, and you're unlikely to acquire one. Even your inability to collect your pet on time can hardly count against you. AusLaw knows perfectly well that you're not free to collect it yourself."

CD frowned and selected two more tracks, blending them skillfully. "If I've no bad marks, then why am I *here,* Grandad?" she burst out.

"Perhaps you might take it as a compliment, Callie," said Galway after a moment's thought.

"A *compliment!* To get stuck here without another Y'Ad in sight?"

Galway smiled slightly. “I know about the common belief that AusLaw is just another BOSS that tosses the dice and sends Y’Ads and M’Ads wherever the dice happen to land.”

“Doesn’t it do that?”

“No, Callie. Just think of the Policam-Assistants. They see everyone and everything, so they’re always chosen from M’Ads of the greatest integrity, like your father, Willan. And perhaps you were chosen to come here because Desert Depot has been declining for years. It needed someone who wouldn’t be content to sleepwalk through the day. It needed a person who was energetic and inventive and would respect the place as it is, as well as work with the BOSS. Maybe AusLaw thought along those lines when it confirmed your appointment out here. Do you understand?”

“I *do* understand what you’re saying, Grandad,” said CD. “But I really don’t understand how you can believe that AusLaw would actually do that. Dad and Mom don’t believe it.”

Galway watched as she exchanged one track with another. “Callie, would you like to know something you probably shouldn’t?”

“No,” said CD. She felt she already had enough on her conscience. She slapped down the final track and snapped the completed disc out of the JDM. “If I reapply for a pet, will you collect it for me?”

Galway nodded. “Certainly, if I can. Would it be possible for you to show me the oasis now? If you have no other duties?”

"I suppose the BOSS can manage alone," said CD reluctantly, "but wouldn't you rather see the souvenir center? There's a good promofilm about the desert..."

"No, thank you," said Galway. "If I want to see the desert, I'll look at the real thing. I don't like holos."

Most of the other tourists were quietly viewing the promofilm, but Sten Hale was standing right outside the music center.

"I wonder why he came back," said CD as casually as she could. "He doesn't like this place very much."

"He doesn't like any place very much," said Galway. "Maybe he wants to see some more of the wildlife and is hoping you will show him."

"Maybe," said CD. "If so, he'll be disappointed. Most of the wildlife stays away from the tourists."

CHAPTER 11

Fur

Galway was very interested in the oasis, and especially in the part CD had played in its construction.

"I wasn't sure AusLaw would allow us to do it," said CD, "because changing the natural landscape is prohibited. The BOSS said it was permitted because the water was here all along. We just let some of it out of the rehydrating tanks. Once the bigger plants are established, we're going to take the shades away, and the BOSS says we can plant some trees at the edges…"

Galway nodded. "And a few years down the road, you'll be able to plant more beyond them, again and again, until this place is a self-replenishing patch of green."

"Yes, only it won't be me who does it," said CD sadly. "I have only a few more months here, unless I get reappointed to this same job." CD knew that was unlikely. Most Y'Ads were moved to new positions at the end of each year. It wasn't until after they reached M'Ad status that their tenures stretched to renewable half-decades rather than twelve-month blocks. Soon, she would have to move on. What would happen to the oasis then? And what would happen to Cat?

"Would you like to stay on here if you could?" asked Galway.

"Yes, I think I would," said CD. "Only, it would be nice if there was some company other than the BOSS."

Galway nodded thoughtfully. "Tell me about the wildlife around here," he invited. "Your mother said something about thorn lizards, I believe?"

"There are quite a few of those," said CD. "And there are hawks and a few little marsupials, and, of course, dingoes."

"Dingoes are not the only desert carnivores," said a sharp voice behind them.

CD jumped, but Galway simply glanced around. "Well, Sten. I was wondering when you'd come out. Callie, I don't know if you've introduced yourselves before, but this is Sen'Cit Sten Hale. He seems to be very interested in the local wildlife, so why don't you tell him about it."

"She already has, on my former visit," said Hale, "but she hasn't told me everything."

"It would take much longer than an hour to tell you everything about the desert, Sen'Cit," said CD as calmly as she could. "There are snakes and dingoes and marsupials. There are three species of wallaby alone."

"The cat," said Hale. "Tell me about the cat."

Galway looked at him blandly. "There are no cats here, Sten. Y'Ad Callista here was expecting delivery of a clone-kit today, but things didn't work out."

"Nevertheless," said Hale, "there is a cat here. Presumably a feral."

"Perhaps you've had a bit too much sun, Sten," said Galway. "You're seeing things."

"No," said Hale. "This Y'Ad has been seeing things. Things that should never have been here. And she hasn't reported them, have you, Y'Ad?"

CD's mind worked frantically. If she agreed, she would be implying there was something to report. If she denied it, she would be lying. "Everybody sees things in the desert, Sen'Cit," she said at last.

"Not everyone has seen a large feral cat, however," said Hale.

"Neither have you," muttered CD.

"I may not have seen it, but I do have conclusive evidence of its existence. And I have a well-founded theory that it has been *your* meddling and AusLaw's slackness that have brought this *thing* to this region."

"What do you mean?" said CD.

"Water," said Hale darkly. "You have changed the face of the desert, and naturally this *feral* has come here to find water."

Galway laughed. "And you've constructed this bit of nonsense from one blurred pawprint that was probably left by a dingo, Sten?"

"Not at all," said Hale. "I have proof." He removed a transparent envelope from the pocket of his blue uniform. "Do you recognize this, Y'Ad?"

"Of course," said CD. "I packed your juke-disc in it when you were here before."

"And *I* packed something else."

"That's your right, Sen'Cit," she said. "You may take what you like so long as it isn't a fitting of Desert Depot, or any material from the desert, of course."

"Any *naturally occurring* material from the desert," corrected Hale. "I know AusLaw, Y'Ad. The question is, do you?" He smoothed the little packet and showed it to CD. "Analysis proved this to be precisely what I suspected," he said. "Cat fur. And since this fur is a color unmatched by any of the clone-kit breeds, it must have come from a feral."

There was an unpleasant silence, then Galway cleared his throat. "The prints you described to me seemed too large to be a cat's."

"But not too large for a desert-feral."

Galway glanced at CD and she broke in quickly. "Desert-ferals were a species developed through natural selection, Grandad. I read about them on my data-disc before I ordered my clone-kit."

"You say 'were'?" said Galway.

"That's right. According to the data-disc, they've been extinct for nearly a hundred years."

"I see," said Galway. He looked blandly at Sten Hale. "I think you must be mistaken, Sten."

"I am *not* mistaken."

The BOSS, disturbed by the raised voices in the oasis, rolled out and informed CD that the solar-bus had been rehydrated and was ready to leave.

"I shall be remaining here," said Sten Hale.

<You are?> said the BOSS.

"Sten Hale. Sen'Cit."

<Purpose for proposed extension of visit?>

"Observance and extermination of a desert-feral," said Hale.

<Desert-feral is a semi-mythical creature. Extinct.> said the BOSS as it scanned the man's retinal print.

"It is here and alive. I have seen the prints. I have collected fur."

There was a long pause, and CD was uneasily aware that the BOSS was trying to formulate another of its nonprogrammed answers. <Desert-feral is a semi-mythical creature. Extinct.> said the BOSS. <A desert carnivore is a dingo. Error to report. Error made in observation.>

"You aren't implying that I might be incompetent, are you, Mark-17?"

There was an even longer pause. <Sen'Cit Sten Hale mistaken about desert-feral. Insufficient data currently available on general competence.> said the BOSS.

Sten Hale gave up on the BOSS and plunged off into the desert, peering into every shadowed hollow and scanning the horizon. CD clenched her hands, convinced that Cat's curiosity would draw it to Sten Hale just as it had been drawn to her.

<Return.> said the BOSS. <Unauthorized, unescorted pedestrian travel in desert prohibited by AusLaw.>

Hearing this, Sten Hale came back to the oasis and insisted on using the vidwindow to contact AusLaw. "I want a permit for desert investigation immediately!" he said as AusLaw appeared on-screen.

<Permit denied.> said AusLaw. <Reboard solar-bus.>

While all this was going on, CD clenched her hands anxiously, hoping that Cat would continue to stay away.

Lone-One had come to accept and even to like the young Two-Leg, but that didn't mean it intended to have any run-ins with an elder Two-Leg, especially one that smelled of bad temper and ill will. Lone-One lay downwind of the intruder, concealed behind a clump of brush and a pile of rocks. Its nose twitched with distaste. It was hungry, but it didn't even consider obtaining full-belly using this elder Two-Leg, who looked so tough and stringy. Besides, the young Two-Leg was at the place of water and was willing Lone-One away as hard as it could. The young Two-Leg was very afraid.

Under direct orders from AusLaw, Sten Hale was forced to board the solar-bus.

"But I'll be back, Y'Ad," he said to CD. "I'll have that permit, and I'll be back."

CD looked nervously at Galway, who simply turned out his hands and gave her a reassuring smile, but she could see the doubt in his eyes. She saw him glancing around, as if half-expecting an extinct animal to amble into the solar-bus park and prove Sten Hale's point. And Cat might easily show up, even yet.

And that's *my* fault, CD told herself starkly. I feed Cat, so it isn't afraid of people anymore. Cat probably even likes them.

For Cat's own safety, she should have chased the desert-feral away from Desert Depot as soon as she saw it. For the safety of the local wildlife, she should have reported its presence that same day. She had made excuses and done neither, and though AusLaw's denial of a permit had bought her a little time, she knew Sten Hale wouldn't give up.

But what could he do? After all, he was only human. He was only a Sen'Cit. What could he do?

CD put her face in her hands. She knew perfectly well what he could do, and she had absolutely no doubt that he would do it.

After the solar-bus departed, Cat returned, and CD wavered. If she fed the desert-feral, it would stay around and become even more of a danger to itself and to her. If she turned it away, it would become more of a danger to the native animals. If she allowed it to spend the night in her quarters, she would be compounding her disobedience. If she did not, it would yowl all night. CD's head spun and ached. Once you started doing wrong, nothing seemed right.

For the next two days, CD went about her duties in a worried daze. She stopped leaving food for Cat, and she didn't allow the desert-feral to sleep in her quarters.

She often found herself shaking, and it did no good at all to remember that this situation was her own fault.

In all her years as a Pr'Ad, she had had nothing to fear from anyone or anything. AusLaw said that all citizens had the right to material support and comfort and safety. The only thing required in exchange was obedience. It was simple, it was logical, and it was right. AusLaw's creed was so obviously sensible that no one in their right mind would disobey: Do no harm, and do not, through action or inaction, allow harm to be done.

She had learned that creed and believed it, but now, in her very first position as a Y'Ad, she had disobeyed. Sen'Cit Sten Hale had found her out, and he was going to report her actions to AusLaw. And AusLaw, her friend and guardian, would be forced to take action against her.

Anxiously, CD wondered what AusLaw would do to her. A shot of sleepygas, and the headache and disorientation it produced, was the usual disciplinary measure used by AusLaw. A blast of sleepygas would stop offenders in their tracks for about an hour, and every time they attempted to do further harm, they would be prevented from doing so by another blast.

But sleepygas was meant to prevent harm, not to punish the offender. Sleepygas wouldn't prevent Y'Ad Callista Derry from harboring the desert-feral. She had done it already. A blast of sleepygas wouldn't make her report her discovery. Someone else would have already reported it. Sleepygas would achieve nothing, so AusLaw probably wouldn't use it. And surely AusLaw wouldn't deregister her for something like this!

CD shivered. A deregistered person was officially dead and could not draw rations. Removed from society, a deregistered human being was provided no food, no clothes, and no status, and was no better off than a feral.

She had shared her rations with the desert-feral. Bleakly, CD wondered if the desert-feral would return the favor.

Lone-One was very hungry. The young Two-Leg was still there, but it did not lay out its usual offering on the stone. Lone-One felt cheated. It had begun to regard the young Two-Leg as a friend and a convenient source of full-belly. It had been pleasant to enjoy thirst-quench so close by. It had also been pleasant to share the young Two-Leg's routine and place of rest. And now all of these comforts had been withdrawn. Lone-One was *not* pleased. Then it began to rain.

<Y'Ad Callista Derry?>

CD stared blankly at the Mark-29 BOSS framed in the vidwindow. She hadn't expected this to happen so soon. Although the past two days of waiting had seemed to stretch on endlessly, CD wished they could have lasted forever.

<You are Y'Ad Callista Derry?> repeated the Mark-29. It was a much more sophisticated BOSS than Desert Depot's resident Mark-17, but CD was in no shape to appreciate the crisp tones in which it spoke.

"Yes," she said listlessly.

<You are summoned by AusLaw to account for your actions regarding an alleged feral animal in your area.> said the Mark-29.

"Summoned? Where?" said CD.

<You will attend an AusLaw coordinate via jet-carrier.>

"But I'm not allowed to leave Desert Depot."

<Who disallows this?>

"Well, AusLaw does."

<Who summons you?>

CD sighed. "AusLaw, and since it *is* the law, it can't do anything illegal."

<Faulty logic.> noted the Mark-29 and signed out.

CHAPTER 12

AusLaw

CD took nothing with her from Desert Depot. There didn't seem much point. There didn't seem much point in ignoring Cat any longer either, so CD left an entire day's rations at the oasis for the desert-feral.

"I might not see you again," she said. Cat looked at her warily for a moment, then turned to rub its furry cheek against her hand.

"If I don't come back…" began CD, but she realized the absurdity of what she had been about to say and shrugged instead. "I can't tell you to run, and you can't draw rations yourself," she said. "I'd ask the BOSS to feed you, but the BOSS thinks you're a dingo, and dingoes are wild, so they don't get rations. Good-bye, Cat."

The giant cat purred and rubbed against her legs. Suddenly, it glanced at the sky, then slid fluidly away.

CD glanced up as well, but it was some time before she could identify the sight and sound of a jet-carrier.

The BOSS pilot of the jet-carrier said nothing, but the human copilot was awake. He was a Y'Ad, and he insisted on telling CD all about jet-carriers.

"Yes, but can you fly it?" she snapped, finally.

"My BOSS is teaching me," he said. "My BOSS says I have initiative. Do you?"

"Yes, unfortunately." CD wondered if he'd talk to her if he knew what she had done.

The jet-carrier's trajectory was short and steep, and very soon CD was disembarking, not in the city, but in a small desert clearing. She got out, and, after a jaunty wave from the Y'Ad copilot, the jet-carrier departed.

CD's spirits sank. She was alone in this place, far from the city, far from Desert Depot. Perhaps she had been deregistered already. She sat down, clasped her hands tightly around her knees, and waited for whatever would happen next.

<You are Y'Ad Callista Derry?> said a voice behind her.

A white pillar with a vidwindow screen displaying the round blue dome of AusLaw had emerged from the sand and rocks.

"Yes," she said dismally. "Am I deregistered?"

<You are here to answer, not to ask.>

"I see," she said sullenly.

<Why are you here?>

"To answer."

<Why are you here?>

AusLaw was endlessly patient and would continue to ask the same questions until it had the right answer, so CD sighed and made the proper response. "Because AusLaw sent for me."

<Why did AusLaw send for you?>

"I expect it's because Sen'Cit Sten Hale has filed a report that I broke AusLaw."

<Did you?>

"Yes," said CD.

AUSLAW

<Why?>

"I don't really know."

<Was it for personal gain?>

"No. Yes. Oh, I don't know," said CD miserably.

<Explain.>

"There's a feral animal at Desert Depot, and I didn't report it."

<Explain from the beginning.>

"I asked for a job with animals or music," said CD. "The C'Off sent me to Desert Depot. At first I was disappointed. The BOSS wouldn't let me use the JDM unless a tourist wanted a mixed disc, and none of them did. I was lonely. I took my exercise in the desert, and I realized there was something out there watching me. When I finally got a look at it, I didn't know what it was. It looked like a cat, but when I accessed my data-disc, the only description I could find that fit what I'd seen was that of a desert-feral. The data-disc said they've been extinct for a long time, so I thought maybe it wasn't one after all."

<Why did you not report this?>

"I didn't know for sure," said CD, twisting her hands. "But there were the dingoes, too. Dingoes are allowed, and they're not really native to Australia. You don't have to report dingoes."

<Human beings are not really native to Australia, and dingoes have existed in Australia for almost as long as human beings. Logic dictates that to disallow dingoes is to disallow human beings.>

"Oh," said CD. "BOSS-logic again."

<Continue.>

"I wanted to be outside to see more of the cat-thing so I began making an oasis. You know about that. You issued the permit. The BOSS saw the cat-thing, but the BOSS doesn't believe in desert-ferals, so it didn't make a report. The cat liked the oasis, and after I began to give it some of my rations…"

<You gave it rations?>

"Yes. It was hungry and I thought it wouldn't eat the wildlife if I fed it. It started coming for food every day, and it started spending the nights in the oasis. When it rained, I opened my window and it came in and slept in my quarters. It likes that, and now it doesn't want to sleep outside in the desert."

<You give it rations. You allow it to sleep in your quarters. Did you also give it a name?>

CD flushed hotly at the implied sarcasm. "I call it Cat," she muttered.

<And where is this Cat right now?>

"Probably asleep in my quarters," said CD. "The window is open and I left it some extra rations."

There was a short silence. When the questions began again, they took a different tack.

<According to your record, you applied for a permit to keep a pet cat.>

"Yes, but…"

<Correct?>

"Yes."

<Your order for a rex clone-kit was approved, Y'Ad, yet your record indicates that you never took delivery of this order. Correct?>

"Yes."

<Why?>

"I couldn't get to the city, so I put the order on hold. When my grandfather went to collect it, the order had been canceled. I meant to reorder, but I suppose I won't be allowed to now," CD said bitterly.

<Correct.>

"And it's all because I didn't report a feral animal."

<There is no feral animal.>

"I guess that means you've exterminated it already."

<Define "feral animal," Y'Ad.>

"It's a domestic animal that has gone wild," said CD, her voice wobbling. "It's an animal that should be a pet, but isn't."

<Define "pet," Y'Ad.>

"A pet is a domestic animal cared for by a human being who takes full responsibility for its comfort and behavior." CD's brain was working furiously. "A pet is fed by its owner. The owner provides a place for it to sleep and keeps it company and gives it a name and keeps it out of mischief."

<A remarkably full and accurate description.>

CD's clenched hands relaxed and she smiled. "It should be," she said carefully. "I've just realized that I already have a pet myself. It's big and orange and I call it Cat. And since I have a pet already, I can't reorder that rex clone-kit!"

<Correct.>

"But, does this mean I'm not in trouble after all?" she said incredulously.

<No. You have not respected AusLaw.>

CD's face fell. "What is going to happen to me?" she asked.

<Appropriate disciplinary measures must be taken. Sleepygas is inappropriate. Deregistration is inappropriate. AusLaw provides for individual treatment of some cases. Yours is such a case. You will now receive a caution.>

"A caution?" CD stammered.

<You will return to Desert Depot and continue to develop the oasis. You will care for your pet cat, which will now receive appropriate rations. You will continue to greet tourists. At the end of the year, you will be granted two weeks of leave, after which your appointment will be renewed. At this point, three more Y'Ads will be assigned to duty at Desert Depot. You will continue to demonstrate initiative and self-reliance and encourage the other Y'Ads to do likewise. You will ***not*** continue to demonstrate further disobedience. In order to keep the oasis vegetation safe from overbrowsing and wildlife safe from your pet cat, an area of one square kilometer will be skyfenced around Desert Depot. Do you accept this caution, Callie?>

CD tried hard to look suitably chastened, but she could scarcely keep from smiling with complete surprise. "Yes," she said, and smiled directly at the vidwindow. "Yes, AusLaw, I accept the caution you have provided. But, how do I get back to Desert Depot?"

<Transport will be provided.>

Within a few minutes, a jet-carrier arrived. This time, the copilot was not a talkative Y'Ad but Galway Derry. CD was not surprised. "Hello, Grandad!" she said, grinning. "Are you enjoying your peaceful Sen'Cit life that is free from any responsibilities?"

Galway coughed. "Let's just say it's not as peaceful as I was once led to believe," he said, with a small smile.

"Why do you let everyone believe AusLaw is a sort of BOSS?"

"That's what they *want* to believe," said Galway.

"Do Ashlin and Willan believe it?"

"Of course, Callie. *Everyone* believes it, except AusLaw, and AusLaw doesn't talk."

"You just did."

Galway held up his hand. "Wait a minute! I hope you haven't run away with the ridiculous idea that *I* am AusLaw!"

"Aren't you?" she said uncertainly. "Oh, I suppose you can't be. AusLaw's been around forever. But I don't understand! You must have *something* to do with it. AusLaw just called me 'Callie,' and you're the only one who ever does that."

"I am not AusLaw, but I *am* part of the current AusLaw. One-twentieth, to be exact," said Galway.

"Why? How?"

"It's a long story, Callie. AusLaw was, at one time, precisely what you've always thought it to be," said Galway. "Before that, it was a democratically elected human government. Both versions had their advantages, but there were too many problems.

"With a human government, elected by the general population, laws were often made because politicians hoped to win favor or power rather than because the laws would be good for everyone. It was obvious that the system wasn't working well, so it was changed.

"Since electronic brains can't lie, and have no real reason to seek favor or power, it was decided that an electronic brain would make the best impartial government, and AusLaw was built. Unfortunately, that didn't work very well, either. Computers are *too* logical. They love facts, but they lack imagination. So, early this century, a hybrid was formed as a compromise."

"What sort of hybrid?" asked CD suspiciously.

"AusLaw is now logic combined with imagination, an electronic brain paired with a syndicate of twenty Sen'Cits elected by secret ballot among themselves. Sen'Cits were chosen because it was presumed they would have experienced both dependency and responsibility, and would have the experience and the time to return something of value to the community. Every time a Sen'Cit retires from the AusLaw syndicate, the remaining nineteen elect a new Sen'Cit to replace the retired one. The secret is kept so well that the elections come as a complete surprise – not to say a total shock – to the Sen'Cits elected."

"What if you don't want to be part of AusLaw?" asked CD.

Galway smiled wryly. "We've all been conditioned into complete obedience so well that we never even think of refusing!

"Major public pronouncements are made by the electronic portion of AusLaw – the Mark-5000 – while individual judgments are made by the human portion, speaking through a voice modifier. BOSSes, policams, and certain senior M'Ads keep order."

"If all this is such a secret, why have you told me? Just because you slipped up and called me 'Callie' when you cautioned me?"

Galway shook his head. "Not at all. To put it quite bluntly, you have been part of an experiment, Callie. You see, over the past decade, there has been a growing feeling in the AusLaw syndicate that the kind of blind obedience AusLaw requires can be almost as dangerous as no government at all. So, very slowly, we're changing our orientation."

"By Project Human Touch?"

"Exactly. Through PHT we hope to reestablish the concept of humans doing most of the actual work, and taking responsibility for their own decisions, just as the AusLaw syndicate is doing. It's difficult to change the habits and conceptions of a lifetime, so AusLaw is concentrating its efforts on Y'Ads such as yourself. Whenever promising Y'Ads leave school, we try to place them in challenging situations. Away from policams and school, Y'Ads such as yourself have a choice between blindly obeying the BOSS and using initiative to improve their situations for themselves *and* others. That is what you did when you made the oasis at Desert Depot."

"Did AusLaw know about Cat all along?" asked CD. "Was Cat a part of this experiment?"

"No, the desert-feral came as a complete surprise. You broke all the rules on that one, but fortunately you also worked hard to minimize any of the damage you might have done by failing to do your duty. You succeeded in making what could have been a very bad situation better for everyone involved."

"I suppose I did," said CD slowly. "If I hadn't made friends with Cat, either Cat would have been exterminated or the wildlife would have been eaten. Now Cat is safe and so is the wildlife, and I have a pet."

"Yes," said Galway. "But just because you broke AusLaw once and got away with it, don't think you can do it again. Next time it really might mean a dose of sleepygas, or worse. You see, AusLaw really *does* try to improve things."

"Haven't you broken AusLaw by telling me all this?" asked CD.

"How can AusLaw break AusLaw?" asked Galway rather blandly.

"Now you sound just like a BOSS," complained CD. The jet-carrier landed in the solar-bus parking lot and they both disembarked.

"AusLaw still isn't perfect," said Galway, following CD into Desert Depot, "and perhaps it never will be. The balance between the rights of the individual and the good of the many is almost impossible to achieve."

"Nothing's perfect, but some things come close," said CD, opening the door to her quarters. "Come and meet Cat, but be careful. I haven't told it yet that it's no longer a desert-feral."

<Desert-feral is a semi-mythical creature. Extinct.> remarked the BOSS, rolling up behind them. <Welcome, Y'Ad Callista Derry. Welcome, Sen'Cit Galway Derry, A'L.>

"Hi, BOSS," said CD. "Maybe you'd better come in, too, and meet my pet."

Lone-One sat up and yawned as the young Two-Leg and Cold-One entered with an elder Two-Leg. Cold-One smelled as inedible as ever, and the elder Two-Leg was friendly and did not represent any danger. The young Two-Leg was happy and no longer afraid. Lone-One curled up again. It had full-belly and was warm and comfortable. It was no longer Lone-One. It was Cat. This was a good situation – not perfect, but close.

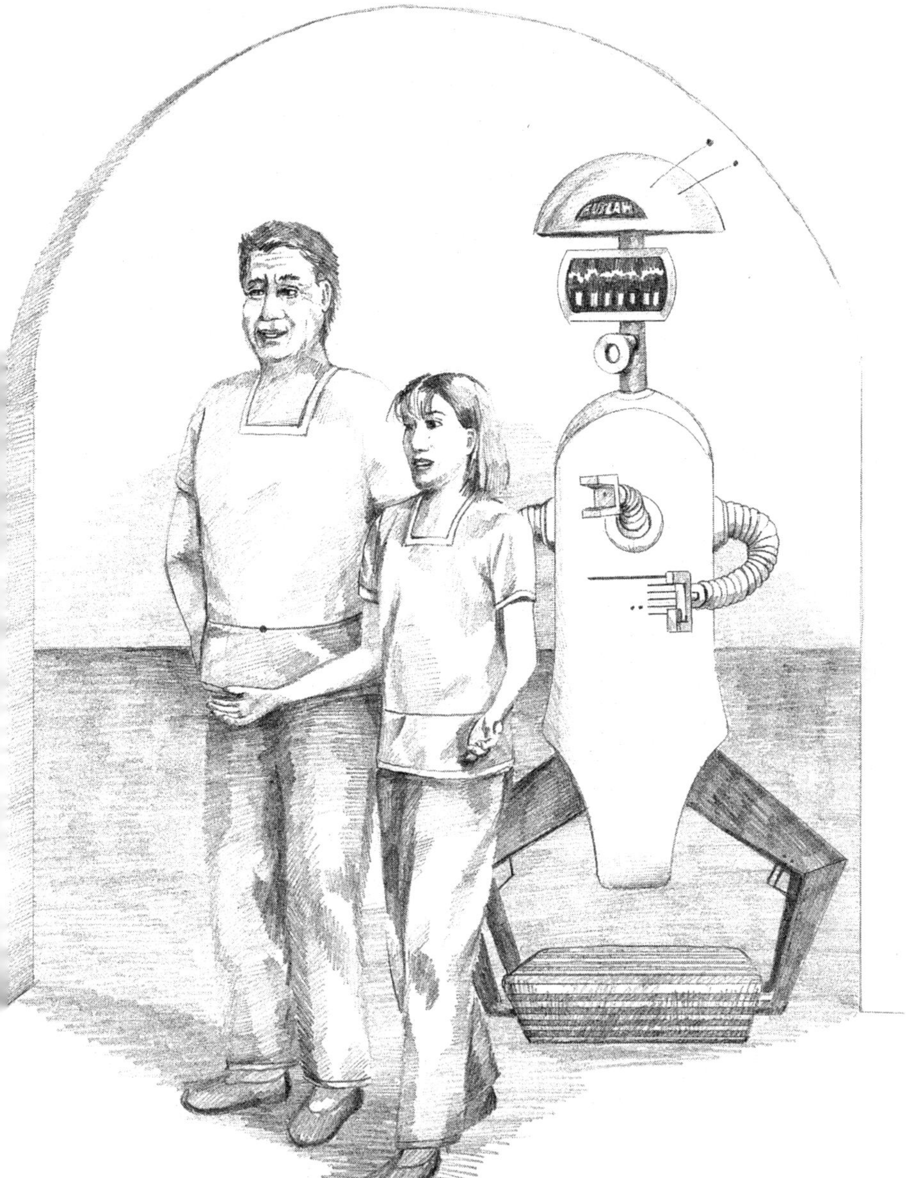

Glossary of Terms

AusLaw – A system of government that provides its citizens with all material needs in return for absolute obedience

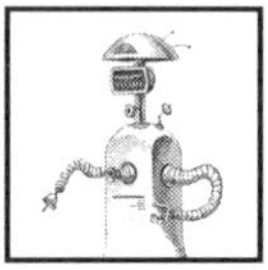

BOSS (Bio Over-SeerS) – A series of robots that regulate human behavior for AusLaw and do most of the real work

breedbanks – Breeding centers in which cloned pets are produced

clone-kit – A cloned cat, one of the six currently available breeds

C'Off (City Career Officer) – A M'Ad who allots preassigned jobs to Y'Ads as part of Project Human Touch

cue-screen – A screen that provides information and answers to C'Offs and other M'Ad workers

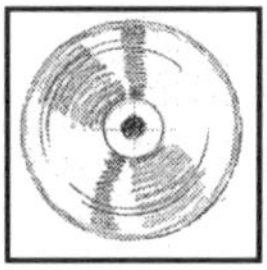

data-disc – An informational CD-ROM

deregistration – The withdrawal of all of an individual's rights and privileges by AusLaw, creating the status of "nonperson"

desert-feral – An oversized feral cat, long thought extinct, that lives in the desert

Eld – An elderly person, at least eighty years old, who wears a yellow uniform and has no responsibilities

highriser – A very tall building divided into separate family dwellings

holo-poster – A holographic poster used for decoration, information, education, or entertainment

JDM (Juke-Disc-Mix equipment) – The machine on which music is selected and then recorded on juke-discs

jet-carrier – A small flying vehicle reserved for official travel or transport

juke-disc – A CD-ROM on which music is mixed, stored, and played

Kid – An infant, up to six years old, who is dressed in an orange uniform and kept under parental care

M'Ad – A mature adult, eighteen to sixty years old, who wears a red uniform, is obliged to work, and may marry and have one child

plasticrete – A synthetic combination of plastic and concrete used in building construction

policam – A police camera used for protective surveillance

Pr'Ad – A preadult, six to twelve years old, who wears green uniforms, undergoes compulsory schooling, and is under parental care

Project Human Touch (PHT) – An AusLaw initiative that places people in jobs as an exercise in human relations

promofilm – An educational or informational promotion holograph

Sen'Cit – A senior citizen, sixty to eighty years old, who wears a blue uniform, possesses more freedom, and may travel

sleepygas – An instant sleeping gas used to prevent crime and other antisocial behavior

solar-bus – A very old-fashioned solar-powered vehicle used for tourism by Sen'Cits

speed-rail – A form of convenient high-speed public transport

vidwindow – A communication device that relays sound and images

Y'Ad – A young adult, thirteen to eighteen years old, who wears a brown uniform, is obliged to work, but receives privileges such as pets

Glossary of "Cat Speak"

Cold-One – a BOSS

Lone-One – Cat's name for itself

Flying-One – bird

Slithery-One – snake

Full-belly – well-fed, a full stomach

Thirst-quench – water

Hopping-One – marsupial

Two-Leg – human

Evolution of Desert-Ferals

ca. A.D. 1800	Cats are introduced into Australia.
ca. 2000	Farms fail in area of the Great Stone Desert. Farm cats become feral, and weaker breeds die out.
2003	Tigers become extinct. Attempts to preserve tiger DNA begin, employing genetic engineering.
2015	"Tigats," a mixed breed of domesticated cats and tigers created through genetic engineering, are created as an offshoot of the tiger DNA-preservation program.
2022	Genetic engineering of animals outlawed. All tigats reportedly destroyed. Evidence of tigat experimentation never released to public.
2023	A load of surviving tigats from a secret compound in the Great Stone Desert escapes after solar-bus transporting them for destruction veers off road and crashes. Tigats and farm ferals interbreed.
2029	A tigat/feral litter is born in which one kitten, "Big Red," shows a mutation of significantly greater size and intelligence.
2053	Desert-ferals, the descendants of Big Red, begin to outcompete remaining farm ferals and tigats and stake claim to interior of the Great Stone Desert.
2120	Desert-ferals well established. Some reports surface of their existence, but they are considered to be mythical creatures.
2197	No desert-ferals reported for fifty years. Creatures are believed to be semi-mythical, and are officially considered extinct.
2279	Desert-feral rediscovered and protected through the actions of Callista "CD" Derry, and are considered for "developed species" status.

From the Authors

We live in Tasmania with our two children, and our entire family loves a good science fiction story. We got the original idea for *CD and the Giant Cat* after Darrel read a newspaper article about large feral cats in Australia. We wondered what might happen if the cats grew even larger. Would they be classified as pests or as a new species? At about the same time, Darrel remarked that it would be great if we could go to a music store and have our own music selections placed on a CD. That way, each track would be a personal favorite. These two ideas came together to create *CD and the Giant Cat*.

Sally and Darrel Odgers

From the Illustrator

I live in Denver, Colorado, with my wife, Penny, and daughter, Averi; two cats, Sly and Yahoo, and a dog named Scooter. I love to draw and paint. Besides illustrating children's books, I also create fine art and work as a commercial graphic designer. I really enjoyed working on *CD and the Giant Cat.* As a pet owner, I can relate to CD's feelings for Cat. Our own cats, in fact, served as models for Cat.

Yahoo and Sly

Tim Lange

Written by **Darrel** and **Sally Odgers**
Illustrated by **Timothy Lange**
Edited by **David Nuss**
Designed by **Pat Madorin**

04 03 02 01 00
11 10 9 8 7 6 5 4 3

Distributed in the United States of America by
Rigby
a division of Reed Elsevier Inc.
P.O. Box 797
Crystal Lake, IL 60039-0797

Printed by Colorcraft, Hong Kong
ISBN: 1-57257-667-7